D1510735

OTHER BOOKS BY ROBERT BAHR

Home Again, Home Again, New Voices in the Southern
   Tradition (editor) Factor Press
Indecent Exposures (anthology of published short fic-
   tion) Factor Press
The Hibernation Response (Arbor House/William Morrow)
Good Hands (New American Library)
Least of All Saints (Prentice-Hall)
The Blizzard (Prentice-Hall)
The Virility Factor (Putnam & Sons)
Man With a Vision (Moody)

DRAMATIC TECHNIQUE
IN
FICTION

by Robert Bahr

Factor Press
P. O. Box 8888
Mobile, Alabama 36689

ISBN: 1-887650-09-1

Publisher's Cataloging-in-Publication Data

Bahr, Robert, 1940-
    Dramatic technique in fiction / Robert Bahr.

    p. cm.

    ISBN 1-887650-09-1
    1. Authorship - Handbooks, manuals, etc.
    2. Fiction - Technique.
    3. Fiction - Authorship.
I. Title.
PN145.B33 1998

Cover photograph courtesy of
Levenger "Tools For Serious Readers" Catalog Co.
Delray Beach, Florida

This book is dedicated to those of my former, current, and future students who understand that art is made through craft, and that craft is passion in harness.

And to my dearest friend, Alice.

CONTENTS

Preface

Although I expect that most people interested in writing will profit by reading this book, its ideal readers are not novices at writing. They've done enough of it to know the problems. They've asked, "Have I described too much?" "How do I make this character believable?" "Which is the ideal voice to narrate the book?" "Where should the work be set?" "Why isn't it *working*?" And countless other questions. These are sophisticated concerns, and can be raised only by experienced writers.

The answers lie in the *conception* of the work. And that's what *Dramatic Technique* offers—clearly and to the point, I hope: an effective way to really understand what you, as a writer, are out to do and why. We begin by putting together a story, choosing a narrator for it, a setting, the characters, a director, the audience. And of course you play every one of those roles yourself.

I cannot guarantee that you will become a great writer because you are reading this book. But I *can* guarantee that you will be a better one—that you will come away from these pages with new—and practical—insight into writing for the satisfaction of the reader. It won't come any easier to you—probably it will be more difficult. But I have taught writing to more than a thousand people during my career as a professional writer, and I am confident that every one of them who has taken the work seriously has saved months, years, perhaps a decade of struggling through that ungodly maze of trial, error, and despair that may eventually lead to effective, quality writing. As you read these pages, you will be taking a shortcut.

All right. Let's get on with it.

CHAPTER I
The Theater of the Imagination

Now, I don't want you to worry about my getting too abstract or theoretical. That's the last thing I'm going to do. But the obvious fact is that you must know exactly what you're trying to do when you write a story. Otherwise you'll do it only by chance.

First, let's elevate ourselves in our own estimation. All stories—even those anecdotes in popular articles—are *art*. It may be high art or low, good art or bad, but literature is an art form—"the production or expression of what is beautiful, appealing, or of more than ordinary significance," including, "skilled workmanship," according to the dictionary. But literary art is different from other art forms. It is unique. *And that uniqueness makes all the difference in what you as a writer are trying to do.*

A sculpture sits on a table or the floor or a pedestal, and the person who stands before it in admiration has visual—sensuous—interaction with it. He may even touch it, caress it.

Museum goers stand one after another before a Van Gogh canvas of swirling orange, blue, white, green. All respond to the immediate, physical impact of the colors and motion on their retinas. The appeal is directly to the senses.

We are in a concert hall. The conductor lifts his wand, and with a flourish of his wrist, the pianist plays the first three notes of Tchaikovsky's Concerto Number One in B Flat Minor, and suddenly the entire orchestra gathers the sweet strains of the piece. The walls fairly shudder under the physical impact of the sound waves, a vibration which touches our ears in a direct, physical, sensuous way.

It's the same whether we watch an opera, a ballet, a dramatic play, a film—such arts appeal directly, physically, to our senses.

Where does the *writer's* art exist? For example, where can you show me the art of a novel? If you hand me the book, I'll say that you're mistaken. And of course you know it already. That book is nothing but row after row, page after page of twenty-six distinct squiggles, upper and lower case, interrupted with various punctuation marks and separated into blocks called paragraphs. Not only is that not art, but many people—especially youngsters—consider it the antithesis of art: so boring in appearance that many intelligent people will hand the book back to you and say, "No thank you. I'll wait for the movie."

You see, the sculptor's marble is the *substance* of his art. So, too, the painter's paint and canvas, the actual sound as the musician creates it, the movement of the dancer's body, the music of the singer's throat. But the *writer*! He has a sometimes maddening handicap. He has to be artist enough to *overcome the medium in which he works*, that sterile, boring page, in order to allow his art to come into existence in the only theater in the world where it can live as literature—*the theater of the reader's imagination.*

Now, isn't that an incredible thought? Literary art does not exist in books. It's locked up in them, yes. But because of its unique nature, that art form which is communicated by the written word is actually experienced only in the minds of the writers and their readers, in their imaginations.

But when a performance succeeds on that theater of the imagination, words transcend their physical existence on the page. They create a unique opportunity which no other art form, even in the hands of its finest masters, can claim: They allow the writer alone to command *all* the arts. While the musician and the composer perform their music for the ear, and the painter and sculptor create their works for the eye, the writer, through words, creates upon the stage of the reader's imagination all the paintings and sculptures and overtures and concertos and operas and ballets of which his talent is capable. He uses not one or two of the senses but all of them.

Listen:

And music! Finished as no music is ever finished. Delete one note and there would be diminishment. Delete one phrase and the structure would fall... Here again was the very voice of God.... I heard the music of true forgiveness filling the theater, conferring on all who sat there perfect absolution.

—Peter Shaffer,
Amadeus

Look:

Eventually they entered a dark region where, from a careening building, a dozen gruesome doorways gave up loads of babies to the street and the gutter. A wind of early autumn raised yellow dust from cobbles and swirled it against a hundred windows. Long streamers of garments fluttered from fire escapes. In all unhandy places there were buckets, brooms, rags, and bottles. In the street infants played or fought with other infants or sat stupidly in the way of vehicles. Formidable women, with uncombed hair and disordered dress, gossiped while leaning on railings, or screamed in frantic quarrels. Withered persons, in curious postures of submission to something, sat smoking pipes in obscure corners. A thousand odors of cooking food came forth to the street. The building quivered and creaked from the weight of humanity stamping about in its bowels.

—Stephen Crane
Maggie: A Girl of the Streets

Feel:

The man's red beard and mustache were likewise frosted, but more solidly, the deposit taking the form of ice and increasing with every warm moist breath he exhaled. Also, the man was chewing tobacco, and the muzzle of ice held his lips so rigidly that he was unable to clear his chin when he expelled the juice. The result was that a crystal beard of color and solidity of amber was increasing its length on his chin...

Once in awhile the thought reiterated itself that it was very cold and that he had never experienced such cold. As he walked along he rubbed his cheekbones and nose with the back of his mittened hand. He did this automatically, and again changing hands. But rub as he would, the instant he stopped his cheekbones were numb. He was sure to frost his cheeks. He knew that, and experienced a pang of regret that he had not devised a nose strap of the sort Bud wore in cold snaps.

—Jack London,
"To Build a Fire"

Smell:

There was a hateful sultriness in the narrow streets. The air was so heavy that all the manifold smells wafted out of the houses, shops, and cook-shops—smells of oil, perfumery, and so forth—hung low, like exhalations, not dissipating. Cigarette smoke seemed to stand in the air, it drifted so slowly away...

...suddenly he noticed a peculiar odor, which, it seemed to him now, had been in the air for days without his being aware: a sweetish, medicinal smell, associated with wounds and disease and suspect cleanliness. He sniffed and pondered and at length recognized it; finished his tea and left the square at the end facing the cathedral. In the narrow space the stench grew stronger. At the street corners placards were stuck up, in which the city authorities warned the population against the danger of certain infections of the gastric system, prevalent during the heated season; advising them not to eat oysters or other shellfish and not to use the canal waters.

> —Thomas Mann,
> *Death in Venice*

That and more is what the written word can achieve. But, to repeat, the writer who holds up a book and says, "This is what I've created," doesn't mean it. All those words, in and of themselves, are nothing. Think of it: the *art* of the writer does not exist *anywhere* in tangible form. Only as his words are transformed into effective theater in the imagination of the reader does the writer's art exist.

When that's understood, we immediately recognize something about writers who tell stories: They're theatrical. Stendhal as a young man moved to Paris to study play writing and frequently attend the theater. Thomas Mann was not much more than ten years old when he began playing with a large, well-equipped puppet theater:

"I would shut myself in alone with it to perform the most wonderful musical dramas," he wrote in "The Dilettante." "The performers would now enter; I had

15

drawn them myself with pen and ink, cut them out and fitted them into little wooden blocks so that they could stand up. They were the most beautiful ladies and gentlemen in overcoats and top hats."

The young Mann spoke the dialogue of each character, sang the background music, "the dull warning rumble of the drums with which the overture began... the horns, clarinets and flutes; these I reproduced with my own voice in inimitable fashion..." He wrote the story line. He applauded when the curtain fell. And he took his well-deserved bow.

Jane Austen was fascinated with the theater. James Joyce studied it seriously. Eudora Welty, one of America's finest short story writers, has said, "I have been a constant movie-goer all my life... And part of my life in New York was spent running out to the Thalia and all those places, every little foreign film place in New York, seeing all those films."

Charles Dickens so loved theater that he produced his own plays and starred in them. One biographer says Dickens would be "stage-manager, often stage-carpenter, scene arranger, property man, prompter, and band master. His correspondence abounds with the deep interest he took in the proceedings, even in the minutest details.... This kind of voluntary hard labor was his great delight."

Virtually all writers, some consciously, most unconsciously and instinctively, have understood the theatrical nature of their art. In fact, the eighteenth century novel was often unabashedly imitative of the play, scene by melodramatic scene, a "stage manager" always standing in full view of the audience to comment on the story. J. B. Amerongen, author of *The Actor in Dickens*, even suggests that the first novels might justly be called plays with lengthy stage-directions.

The successful writer, whether he's aware of it or not, is simultaneously a dramatist, stage manager, actor, set designer, director, and audience. He's responsible for the lighting and furniture, the pacing, the conflict and plot, and for the behavior of each actor who sets foot on the stage. He must lift the curtain, and bring it down. And like the young Thomas Mann, he must take his seat in the audience and observe—laugh and weep, boo and hiss, and when, in spite of his critical and demanding nature, he is pleased, applaud himself.

These are the skills of *dramatic technique* that lead to art. It's not easy. If it were, every manuscript would be a published book, and every book a classic. But it *is* possible, and, that being the case, the serious writer may be compelled to attempt it. Some of you will succeed, and will be the creators of spectacular performances.

Although I call this book *Dramatic Technique in Fiction*, most of what I'll be saying in these pages applies not only to fiction but to what's been called the "new" journalism or "literary fact" as well. "What most contemporary literary writers and critics have not fully realized," say André Fontaine and William A. Glavin, Jr., in *The Art of Writing Nonfiction*, "is that during the last 30 years, a new dimension in journalism has slowly emerged. Today, some of the most vital and creative writing in the English language is being done by journalists."

Actually, the genre has been around a bit longer than 30 years. Charles Dickens wrote literary fact. So did Steven Crane, Mark Twain, George Orwell, Ernest Hemingway, James Agee, and more recently, Truman Capote, Norman Mailer, Tom Wolfe and many others. You'll find examples of it in newspaper features, magazines, and crime books, and of course the true "I remember" pieces.

It's my guess that within a few years most colleges and universities will require courses in literary fact, including such seminal works as Agee's *Let Us Now Praise Famous Men*, Wolfe's *Electric Kool-Aid Acid Test*, Ludwig's *Napoleon*, Capote's *In Cold Blood*, Ekstein's epic prose poem, *The Body Has a Head, a Guide to Human Physiology*. The list goes on.

I'm stressing this matter of literary fact in order to bring some open-minded thinking to those few fiction writers reading these words who are under the delusion that they alone have a corner on dramatic technique. In fact, dramatically recreating true stories is often much more difficult, requiring greater skill, than writing fiction from the ground up. But the techniques are the same.

We'll begin almost immediately, but first I want to make these two final points:

—These chapters unfold in arbitrary order. The very best writing doesn't necessarily begin with a plot, or characters, or a theme, or even purpose. Sometimes they all come at once as an entire package, probably the way a sculptor conceives his work. There's something almost miraculous about that—the sudden "I have it!" when the entire work comes full-blown to the artist—the characters required, the nuances of their nature, the story, the theme. But that's rare. Much more often a story originates with a character who demands a stage on which to play, or a setting, or a moral intention—and I once wrote a short story, "Another Time or Place," simply because that title kept haunting me.

—I'm speaking in generalities. You might well discover exceptions to virtually every point I'll make. With experience, you might find approaches that work better for you than the ones I propose. I *hope* that you'll do that; I hope you'll taste what I offer and not just gulp it down. For all that writing is, it is also observation communicated, and if we all obtained everything in the same way, there would be precious little original writing in the world. These are *my* techniques, and they are as far from inflexible rules as you can get.

Now, let's move into the theater of the mind—that is, a *reader's* mind. We have a stage available, and our job is to make use of it. As we go along we'll be wearing the hats of quite a few theatrical professionals. But one thing is certain: We can't do much without a dramatist. Someone needs to put the whole thing down on paper.

CHAPTER II
The Dramatic Concept

Every writer begins as a dramatist—the one who has the *idea*. "There has to be an idea," says Eudora Welty. "What is alive in it (the work) is this idea." The idea is the very heart of the story, according to Welty, toward which the whole story moves. John Steinbeck called it the "something from writer to reader," which could be reduced to a single sentence. Nothing is more important than the idea, and no one should even begin writing unless he has a clear understanding of it. Yet, the most common failing by far among beginning writers in my experience is the lack of a clear and specific idea.

An idea is not just a subject. *An idea is a subject and a creative intent.* The creative intent—what a writer intends to say about the subject—makes an idea.

Subject	Creative Intent	Idea in Execution
Good and evil.	Sometimes what appears to be good can be evil, and vice-versa	*The Scarlet Letter*, by Nathaniel Hawthorne
Spring break	All my efforts to pick up girls fail	Paper by a pitiful student

Until the late 19th century, the creative intent was called the moral—the lesson or point to be derived. Today, it might be called the argument, slant, or angle.

The creative intent is more than a story line. It's the reason the writer writes. It may be a clear call to action, such as Ayn Rand's *Atlas Shrugged* or Rachael Carson's *Silent Spring*. It may express a perceived truth, like Desmond Morris's *The Naked Ape* or Robert Heinlein's *Stranger in a Strange Land*. It may be intended to edify or to educate or to express a mood or irony. It may seek to entertain. But whatever the writer's intent, *it must be clear to him from the beginning.*

That's the dramatist's first job—to clarify his creative intent—yet, it's a responsibility many nonprofessionals ignore. They're so eager to begin writing that they never clarify in their own minds their singleminded purpose. That lack is instantly obvious, and not just in fiction. Even in feature article writing, in which facts, quotations and anecdotes are intentionally selected and arranged to evoke a specific response, the creative intent must be clear in the writer's mind at the outset.

That's the beacon toward which his efforts will sail. Without it, he may unwittingly meander out to sea, never to reach any meaningful landfall. He may arrive eventually at a port that holds no profit for him. He may even smash his vessel to bits on a shoal and abandon sailing altogether. It's the creative intent— not the *what* but the *why*—that keeps him on course.

Let me make this more emphatic: Not once in my life have I seen or heard about an article, short story, or book worthy of publication that lacked a clear sense of direction, or creative intent. What's more, the most common reason a typical student's work fails to win the appreciation of other students is that it has no overriding purpose. A typical dialogue:

Me: "Interesting. Where did you intend to go with it?"

Student: "Well, I thought I'd tell about the time I..."

Me: "I see. Why should *I* care? What does that story have to say to *me*? What's the point of it? What does it say about life? Why should I want to read your story? Where does it go beyond itself?"

At about that point, eyes glaze over. Occasionally a student will complain, "I don't want to write an allegory or parable or sermon. I just want to tell an entertaining story."

We *both* want her to tell an entertaining story. But let's see what happens without a creative intent.

The story: boy meets girl, boy loses girl, boy regains girl. A true experience, let's say, with all the pathos and heartbreak and ultimate triumph. Written with much attention to detail. Yet, the story unfolds predictably, even monotonously. The reader yawns and says, "Who cares?"

Enter the creative intent, the purpose beyond the story: *There really is justice in the universe.* (I'm arbitrarily inventing that creative intent—it could be anything.) Instantly we have a source of dramatic tension: It's *right* that these people be together. These are good people who have sacrificed their happiness for the well-being and/or happiness of others. Yet, their passion for each other is palpable. When at last they unite, the story takes on an emphatic quality. Because of the creative intent, the story moves steadily toward the uniting and arrives there decisively.

The successful writer doesn't say to himself, "I will write of the Depression and the dust storms," which is nothing more than an empty cocoon of a subject, but, "I will write of how people can survive, if barely, the overwhelming negatives they confront by clinging to the richness of life," as Steinbeck did in *The Grapes of Wrath*. Not, "I will write about Dublin," but, as Joyce did in *Dubliners*, "I will write of how an environment can make corpses of living people."

Story Line

Having understood his creative intent, the writer-as-dramatist turns to the story line—or plot—of his work.

Sometimes that story line is all but imperceptible to the reader. Yet, if the creative intent is the beacon, the story line is the route of navigation that brings the ship to harbor.

Ultimately most successful writers by far chart that seaway before casting off. They know exactly where they're going *before writing word one*.

Long before James Michener, for example, reveals his plans for a book to a research assistant, he has already plotted the story, developed his characters and blocked out the content of every chapter.

Says Katherine Anne Porter, "If I didn't know the ending of a story, I wouldn't begin. I always write my last line, my last paragraph, my last page first."

Jules Verne wrote, "I start by making a draft of a new story. I never begin without knowing what the beginning, middle, and end will be."

Yet, a few beginning writers have whined, "I want the story to just flow, to come on its own, spontaneously. Plotting is an artifice."

Of course, anyone who thinks that art is *not* artifice is deluded. Art is not life. It is the *illusion* of life, shaped and molded in a way that life rarely is. And when it comes to creating a sense of drama, that shaping requires a beginning, middle, and end.

Whether it's fact or fiction, a story, article, or novel, it needs those three vital parts, just as a sculpture needs a top, bottom, and middle. These are the parts which the dramatist must arrange in logical order. And that requires an extraordinary amount of decision making.

Conflict

But—a beginning, middle, and end to *what*? To *conflict*—and I would have added "of course," except that I have read too many of my students' short "stories."

One of the dangers of being experienced in any field is that you take for granted that everyone knows what you know. I can't remember when I did not realize that the seminal ingredient in drama is conflict. That conflict, or clash between opposing forces, generates suspense in the reader. Will the character whom I like (support, identify with) triumph over the villain/

jerk/punk rock star? How will these wonderful people overcome this hideous threat? The suspense, which grows out of the conflict, keeps us reading in search of the resolution.

Obvious, isn't it? It goes without saying—and did, in fact, in my early lectures. Consequently, between one-fourth and one-third of my students submitted "short stories" (actually, meaningless, unconnected details of their lives and that of their relatives) utterly lacking in conflict and suspense. Reading them was torturous boredom.

So, I will take nothing for granted. If you write in your books, underline or highlight the following sentence: *If you have no conflict that leads to suspense and requires a resolution, you have no story. Resolving a conflict in such a way as to dramatize your creative intent is what a story is all about.*

The Beginning

The central conflict of a story should be introduced in the beginning, if possible in the first paragraph. A short while ago, a young woman turned in the following story: A girl in her early twenties accompanies her boyfriend to a Mardi Gras ball where there is dancing, champagne, hors d'oeuvres. Afterward, the man takes her to several bars. Suddenly, very ill from too much alcohol, the woman goes to a rest room and passes out. She awakens next morning on the floor, dressed in some old man's clothing.

She has no purse and no money, so one of the men at the bar gives her five dollars. After considerable difficulty, she returns home with new insight into the kind of man she had been dating.

The story failed because she began it chronologically, going to the Mardi Gras ball, when in fact it should have begun with the conflict and suspense of awakening in utter confusion on the floor of the ladies' rest room. Rewritten, it was a much more engaging, poignant account.

Keep in mind that the first words of a story must compete for the reader's attention with television, film, videos, magazines, books, and who knows what. Only a riveting conflict-promising lead can hold its own against all that. But even before the entertainment glut, the greatest writers always had bold, muscular beginnings.

Notice how promptly Faulkner transports the reader from the real world to the reality of *Light in August* and the mind and situation of Lena:

"Sitting beside the road, watching the wagon mount the hill toward her, Lena thinks, 'I have come from Alabama: a fur piece. All the way from Alabama a-walking. A fur piece.' Thinking *although I have not been quite a month on the road I am already in Mississippi, further from home than I have ever been before. I am now further from Doane's Mill than I have been since I was twelve years old.*"

No reader is going to stop there. Faulkner has us hooked, at least for one more paragraph. We want to know what conflict has drawn Lena so far from home.

Even Homer captures us with the grand tensions and confrontations of the opening paragraph of his *Iliad*:

"Sing, O Goddess, the anger of Achilles, son of Peleus, that brought countless ills upon the Achaeans. Many a brave soul did it send hurrying down to Hades, and many a hero did it yield a prey to dogs and vultures, for so were the counsels of Zeus fulfilled from the day on which the son of Atreus, king of men, and great Achilles first fell out with one another."

Few beginnings are more compelling than Kate Millet's in her true story *The Basement*, in which she talks to the victim of a heinous murder:

"You have been with me ever since, an incubus, a nightmare, my own nightmare, the nightmare of adolescence, of growing up a female child, of becoming a woman in a world set against us, a world we have lost and where we are everywhere reminded of our defeat. What you endured all emblematic of that. That you endured it at the hands of a woman, the hardest thing in the fable, that too. Who else would be so fit to shatter the woman-child?"

Successful beginnings have these qualities in common:

1. They demand attention. That doesn't mean that they're sensational, at least not for the mere sake of sensation. They might express a fascinating idea, or the mode of expression itself might be riveting. Few beginnings surpass this simple one by Jane Austen in *Pride and Prejudice*: "It is a truth universally acknowledged, that a single man in possession of a good fortune, must be in want of a wife." From that lead paragraph, we're involved in the book.

2. They replace the reader's reality with that of the writer. Ideally it seems to me best to *wrench* the reader from his reality into mine. In articles, the writer might rely on the drama of an anecdote. I began "Born to Bike" for *Boys' Life* this way:

"They were 11 seconds from the finish line. Glancing over his shoulder, the lead bicyclist spotted the rider with flaming red hair and bright blue eyes coming up fast on the outside. It was Bruce Donaghy, and there was just one way to slow him down—take the turn wide, forcing Bruce high up the banked track. Ordinarily that's a good strategy.

"But for Bruce Donaghy, it was the opening he needed for an easy win. Instantly he swerved, missing his opponent's rear wheel by a fraction of an inch. Then, in a furious burst of speed, he passed him on the inside and raced to the wire."

In longer works, such as a novel, the writer can establish the literary reality in more leisurely fashion. Note how effectively Ray Bradbury begins his novel *Dandelion Wine*, quickly bringing alive the summer morning:

"There, and there. Now over here, and here...

"Yellow squares were cut in the dim morning earth as house lights winked slowly on. A sprinkle of windows came suddenly alight miles off in dawn country.

"Every one yawn. Every one up."

Such words as "now," "here," "this," and such take the reader quickly from his reality into the writer's. Writing in the present tense has the same effect, although it can be overdone.

3. The first paragraphs of successful beginnings also set the tone, the mood of the work. Robert Ardrey begins *The Hunting Hypothesis* by putting the human species against a background of time and eternity:

"Why is man man? As long as we have had minds to think with, stars to ponder upon, dreams to disturb us, curiosity to inspire us, hours free for meditation, words to place our thoughts in order, the question like a restless ghost has prowled the cellars of our consciousness.

"Why is man man? What forces divine or mundane delivered to our natural world, that natural creature, the human being? No literate, civilized people, or illiterate primitive tribe has failed to heed the ghost. The question inhabits us all, as universal in our species as the capacity for speech. Did we enter this world carried out of some primal forest on the back of some sacred elephant? Were we coughed up on a pebbly shore by a benevolent, immaculate fish? How frequently, in our oldest myths, the animal participated in the Creation. Even the garden called Eden had its snake."

4. The beginning clearly establishes the narrative voice. (The narrative voice, as we will discuss later, is that of the person telling the story—and it is never you, the writer.) A particularly fine example is the beginning of Bernard Malamud's short story "The Jewbird":

"The window was open so the skinny bird flew in. Flappity-flap with its frazzled black wings. That's how it goes. It's open, you're in. Closed, you're out if that's your fate. The bird wearily flapped through the open kitchen window of Harry Cohen's top-floor apartment on First Avenue near the lower East River."

5. The ideal beginning has in it a hint of the work's creative intent. This isn't always possible, but when it can be accomplished, it intensifies the *unity*, or tied-togetherness of the work.

One of the best examples of this sort of lead—one which reflects the creative intent and the conclusion—is Christopher Isherwood's *A Single Man*:

"Waking up begins with saying *Am* and *Now*. That which has awoken then lies for a while staring up at the ceiling and down into itself until it has recognized *I*, and therefrom deduced *I am, I am now*. *Here* comes next, and is at least negatively reassuring; because *here* this morning, is where it has expected to find itself: what is called *at home.*"

What makes this so effective is the depersonalization of the narrator: "That which has awoken...down into itself until it has recognized..." The human relating the story is coming up from the nonexistence of sleep into life, and finally, into humanity. After a rather ordinary day made extraordinary through a uniquely human capacity to feel passion, the narrator returns to bed, to depersonalization and the ultimate reality of death. From the very first paragraph we understand that we live every moment in a framework of inevitable extinction, and yet, not ignoring that truth, life is still to be celebrated.

The Middle

A good *beginning* catches the reader's attention; a good *middle* keeps it. Professional writers realize that holding attention is critical to success. They no more make excuses for boring readers than surgeons do for causing a patient's death. (Regrettably, literary malpractice is not punishable.)

The writer's responsibility, both to his reader and to his own creative intent, is to be a skillful "entertainer." That's not *all* he is—but he most certainly is that, and those writers who have entertained us best— Shakespeare, Twain, Stevenson, Dickens, and such— are likely to be read long after more sophisticated and less enjoyable authors are but footnotes in literary history.

The usual means of entertaining is to tell a story (fact writers call it an anecdote). A couple of decades ago, Malcolm Cowley wrote, "No doubt remains that story telling has lost the privileged place it used to hold in the publishing world and some of the attention it received from critics as well as readers. Magazines have been printing less and less fiction, and there is hardly a book reviewer who has not announced that the novel is dead." Stories were no longer serious, and did not speak to the age; "plot, which is the story element, is a shameful concession to the audience."

The thinking Cowley described produced a brief flutter of absurdism in the arts. Craftspersons who saw life as meaningless tried to express their views to the public in immortal art, which is an inconsistent thing for an absurdist to do. Andy Warhol, who managed to make substantial profit from meaninglessness, published a volume called, *a*, which was reviewed in the January 12, 1969, issue of *The New York Times Book Review* as follows:

"It consists of 24 hours of talk—there are strangely few silences—tape recorded from the life of Ondyne, a Warhol sidekick who is homosexual, high on amphetamines, and loquacious....

"*a* is not ultimately even realistic. Most of it—because the tape didn't pick up connecting pieces of conversation—is incomprehensible snippets and gobbets of talk. Because Ondyne's brain seems irretrievably addled with amphetamines, most of what he says takes the form of grunts, squeals, and bad puns."

These nonstories of the 1960's and 1970's, with their nonplots and noncharacters, and nonmeanings, have ended up, virtually without exception, with the nonreaders they deserve. And not because the critics have condemned them but because the public—that great mass of farmers and truck drivers, nurses and secretaries, housewives, teachers, business people, those who read literature—simply would not buy it.

People live and suffer, and have firsthand knowledge of life and suffering. They understand futility and even cosmic absurdity. They understand it so well, in fact, that they prefer not to dwell upon it. Instead, they would like to turn away from it for awhile, to catch their breath. Some turn to religion, others to art, including the literary arts. Few have made this point as well as Maren Elwood:

"We see causes without visible effects and effects without visible causes. Life stretches into infinity on either side of us. Our past is bounded by approximately 5,000 years of recorded history. Our vision of the future is no farther away than our next breath, and not always that far. Life does not satisfy the craving for pattern, for logical arrangement that is inherent in our every fiber. Only in the art of the writer can we find satisfaction for this fundamental craving of the human heart for orderly events, for a comprehensible sequence of cause and effect, for unity in character, and for a series of related happenings increasing in dramatic intensity [i.e., conflict], climax and a conclusion."

Entertainment is not a dirty word. Neither is commercial. "I don't write commercial books," a young man told me recently at a writer's conference. "I write serious, literary novels." Having had the misfortune of struggling through a few such unpublished "serious" novels, I'm persuaded that the word often denotes formless rambling, angry diatribe, and the "Watch me! Watch me!" of infancy. That they're not commercial is no virtue. They are not commercial because no one will publish them, and no one will publish them because no one will read them. And no one will read them because *they do not entertain.*

It's not by accident that peasants, along with intellectuals, acclaimed the plays of Shakespeare, that the masses loved Dickens and Twain and Chaucer and Homer. Many of their works have been made into motion pictures in which entertainment is often the primary objective.

E. M. Forster has written, "Scheherazade avoided her fate because she knew how to wield the weapon of suspense—the only literary tool that has any effect on tyrants and savages. This is the fundamental aspect without which it could not exist." The same is true of literary fact. The story—that's entertainment.

The writer who doesn't entertain is a journalist, or perhaps a philosopher, or a preacher or propagandist. He is not an artist, for the literary artist-as-dramatist understands intuitively that he is as much in the entertainment business as Michelangelo, Mozart, and Flaubert were. To entertain is not a creative intent, an overriding purpose of the work. It's a means to an end—but the effectiveness of that end often depends upon the degree to which the reader has been entertained.

The middle of the work is where the writer develops the conflict. Depending on his story and creative intent, he might do this through very gentle, poignant exchanges. Or, if he is writing *Terminator Twenty*, he might have his villain blow up three-quarters of Manhattan. In any case, the middle of the story brings the conflict more intensely into focus, and that *stimulates emotional response both in the characters and the reader*.

That's how literature entertains—through feelings, passions.

The writer-as-dramatist must see his idea, its beginning, middle and end, in emotional rather than intellectual terms. We aren't entertained by a recitation of events. That's news. I could tell you, for example, that a four-year-old boy plunged his tricycle through a glass patio door and almost bled to death, but that his life was saved through a blood transfusion from his ten-year-old sister. It's an interesting but easily forgettable story. Then I could add some emotional detail: The girl, whose name was Cindy, was taken from her fifth grade music class and rushed to the hospital. There, her parents explained that her brother Bobby could survive only with a transfusion of the rare blood type that she alone had.

"Do you understand?" her mother asked.

Cindy nodded. "Okay," she agreed somberly.

For several minutes she lay on the stretcher next to her brother watching the blood move through the plastic tube from her arm to his. Finally, her eyes watered.

"Does it hurt?" her mother asked.

"No," the girl answered. "I just wonder... how long before I die?"

Emotion is the common medium of the arts. The writer may present it with the restraint of a Hemingway in "A Clean, Well-Lighted Place," in which an old man, failing at suicide, stoically awaits death through natural causes, or in the more demonstrable, melodramatic fashion of a Poe in "The Masque of the Red Death." But in both cases, the goal is emotional response.

Hemingway himself made that point when asked, "What would you consider the best intellectual training for the would-be writer?" He answered, "Let's say that he should go out and hang himself because he finds that writing well is impossibly difficult. Then he should be cut down without mercy and forced by his own self to write as well as he can for the rest of his life. At least he will have the story of the hanging to commence with."

Hemingway was saying, in effect, that good writing isn't a display of intellectual proficiency but emotion, passion. That's what we write about.

Robert Louis Stevenson, referring to the dramatic novel, said:

It is sometimes supposed that the drama consists of incident. It consists of passion which gives the author his opportunity.... A good serious play [note that Stevenson equated the dramatic novel with theater] must therefore be founded on one of the passionate *cruces* of life, where duty and inclination come nobly to the grapple; and the same is true of what I call, for that reason, the dramatic novel....

...passion is the be-all and end-all, the plot and the solution, the protagonist and the *deus ex machina* in one. The characters may come anyhow upon the stage, we do not care; the point is that before they leave it they shall become transfigured and raised out of themselves by passion. It may be part of the design to draw them with detail, to depict a full-length character, and then behold it melt and change in the furnace of emotion. But there is no obligation of the sort; nice portraiture is not required, and we are content to accept more abstract types, so they be strongly and sincerely moved. A novel of this class may even be great and contain no individual figure; it may be great, because it displays the workings of the perturbed heart and the impersonal utterance of passion; and with an artist of the second class, it is indeed even more likely to be great, when the issue has been thus narrowed and the whole force of the writer's mind is directed to passion alone.

That's not to say that there aren't excellent stories of setting, of circumstance, or of character. Nonetheless, emotion holds the reader and makes such works effective: "When the passions are introduced into art at their full height," said Stevenson, "we look to see them, not baffled and impotently striving, as in life, but towering above circumstance and acting substitutes for fate."

Thomas Mann makes the same point through Mynheer Peepercorn in *The Magic Mountain*: "I repeat, that therein lies our duty, our sacred duty to feel. Feeling, you understand, is the masculine force that rouses life. Life slumbers, it needs to be roused, to be awakened to a drunken marriage with divine feeling. For feeling, young man, is godlike. Man is godlike, in that he feels. He is the feeling of God. God created him in order to feel through him. Man is nothing but the organ through which God consummated his marriage with roused and intoxicated life. If man fails in feeling, it is blasphemy; it is the surrender of his masculinity, a cosmic catastrophe, an irreconcilable horror—"

All right, in the theater of the mind, the dramatist utilizes entertainment to achieve his creative intent, and entertainment is achieved by evoking emotional response. Whether it is the terror of a horror story, the bittersweet sorrow of *Love Story*, the courage and pride of Scarlet O'Hara, or the brief ecstasy of Francis Macomber, the dramatist seeks out a logical development that *offers the fullest possible opportunity for emotional expression.* The literary dramatist does not want his reader to say, "This is what I *think* about this," but rather, "This is what I *feel.*"

Real feelings come from real people—characters —and we'll talk about where they come from later. Here we're concerned with the work of the dramatist. He must decide not who the characters *are*, but what they *do* and *feel.* If not, he is a failure.

What they *should* do is *confront*—confront circumstances and each other—and respond to those confrontations, those conflicts with the emotions that we all share. That sounds simple, but, especially for beginning writers, all too often it proves impossible. "Too many authors," says Irving Wallace, "will avoid what threatens to be an impossibly difficult scene, although an obligatory scene, and instead will write around it rather than into it, simply from fear that they do not possess the perception or skill to master it. This detour into exposition or past tense or summary, as a substitute for daring to dramatize or play out a crucial confrontation, may be entirely unconscious. But once the fear is understood, and once the work in progress dominates the writer and drives him into the big hell, the author has the chance to live up to his potential."

The conflict can be as subtle as a Pinter play or as grand and detailed as the Battle of Borodino in *War and Peace.* The specifics of the emotion-generating conflict go hand in hand with the guiding beacon of creative intent. Ideally, the dramatist sees it whole—the peaks and valleys of dramatic conflict throughout the logical development of the work, the broad sketch of characters who will make these conflicts most emphatic, the point at which the story begins and ends *emotionally*, rather than literally.

The End

The stories that I like best, and enjoy writing most, end at or very close to the climax—at the point where the story is resolved. In a short story of mine called "Another Time or Place," high school sophomore Robbie Walker watches his best friend drive out of his life forever on a motorcycle and at last gets the courage to yell, "I love you, Crusher." That's how the story ends. In another, "Through a Glass Darkly," little Michael Reemer learns that he will die some day like everyone else, and, conquering his terror, he makes his attempt at immortality by writing, "Once upon a time there lived a boy named Michael Reemer..." And so that story ends. O'Henry and many others ended their stories at the moment when the conflict is resolved—the climax.

Many great stories taper off after the climax in order to resolve loose ends. It's a decision that the literary artist makes based on his material and intent. The standard: Does it work? Does it leave a sense of satisfaction, fulfillment? Does it *work*? Do the beginning, middle and end hold together as a single, complete piece?

This is the rough labor which the writer-as-dramatist must block out clearly before the writing begins. He must be able to say, "Here is what this is all about. We will begin the show at this point, touch these emotion/conflict-stirring peaks along the way, reach this resolution and conclude in this fashion. If he is not lazy, if he does his job well, perhaps what began as a simple recollection of a childhood moral dilemma, a passing glance from a stranger, a word overheard in an elevator, or a brief story in a newspaper may end up being literature.

But it cannot be achieved without discipline. Discipline drives the skilled writer to do a great deal more work *before* he starts putting words on paper than after. Typically, the actual writing is the *least difficult* aspect of the work. As you'll see in later chapters, the writing itself often unfolds rather smoothly when the foundations are in place. The rigorous labor must be done up-front by the writer-as-dramatist. The urge to kick off restraints and plunge head-long into putting words on paper must be resisted by the seriously intentioned. *Art is the product of discipline*, discipline sometimes so unrelenting as to leave its scars on the personalities of the artists themselves. This is the pain you have read about, the travail of the creative process. It is no myth. It is simply not a part of most amateurs' experience, which goes a long way toward explaining the amateurs' status.

CHAPTER III
A Narrative Voice

At the beginning of Thornton Wilder's *Our Town*, the stage manager carries onto an empty stage a table and some chairs. For a moment he observes the audience, then announces, "This play is called *Our Town*.... The name of the town is Grover's Corners, New Hampshire..." Although he's not a participant in the story that the play tells, he appears throughout as its narrator, directing our attention, explaining, interpreting. And when, after three acts, he closes the play, winding his watch and announcing, "You get a good rest, too. Goodnight," we realize that this play about George and Emily, their parents, relatives, and neighbors from first to last has been the *stage manager's*. We've seen it through his eyes and his eyes only.

Every skilled writer, whether consciously or not, tells his story through a "stage manager" who is as much a fiction as a character in a novel. Many beginning writers struggle with the question, "What is my own style, my own voice?" It's an all but meaning-less question. The writer—as *himself*—is not going to be telling the story. His stage manager will be telling it. If you can recognize that fact now, at the outset, it will take an enormous burden off your shoulders as an author, especially if you have limited experience with narrative voice and point of view.

Those unfamiliar with fact writing techniques may be surprised to find that articles, essays, nonfiction books and even letters are written in the voice of a fictional persona or stage manager. This is so important, yet so subtle, a point that I'm reserving it for discussion later. For now I'll be using examples taken from fiction.

Here are the commonly used narrative voices:

1. *Participating, First person.* When Mike Hammer describes crashing through doors in a hail of bullets, no one seriously believes that writer Mickey Spillane once worked as a private detective under the pseudonym Mike Hammer and is telling the true story of his life. Obviously the narrative voice belongs to a fictional character, a stage manager who is also a participating hero who is telling us his story. We hear not a peep from the lips of the real writer.

Literature offers many such examples—Henry James's *The Turn of the Screw*, Poe's "Tell-Tale Heart" among them. The device is very effective when the author wants to delude or mislead the reader. A participating narrator can be as bonkers as a coo-coo bird or as deceitful as a con artist.

Note the gentle, velvety quality of this scene from *A Walk in the Spring Rain* by Rachel Maddux. It features a woman in her fifties, a man about the same age, and two goats. The narrator is not Maddux but the fictional woman of the story. Written from any other perspective it would have been hopelessly syrupy.

"Oh they [the goats] are lovely," I said. "I can't remember when anything has been so satisfying." And in a rush of love I gathered the brown one to me and kissed it.

"I suppose you got a word for that," he said.

"For what?"

"For the way you love them goats," he said. "For the soft hand."

"Oh, tenderness I suppose," I said, feeling my eyes suddenly burn with the excess I know myself to have of it, so that I would pour it out on strangers if it were not that I know that they would call the police or turn from me in fear. It has grown so much greater in me in the last years, this awful flood. In railway stations it's the worst, I think. People look so tired there, so lost sometimes. Oh, isn't it sad that in our world it is so hard to get it? God knows people need it. The faces of young men so often show how terribly they want it. Yet, alas, they all want it from Marilyn Monroe.

2. *First person observer.* Here's the passive narrator. He's part of the story, but not at the heart of the action—and sometimes he does no more than relate the action from his own perspective. Nick Caraway is a comparatively uninvolved character in Fitzgerald's *The Great Gatsby*, but through his eyes Fitzgerald can

make moral observations on the life and values of Jay Gatsby that would be didactic from an omniscient narrator.

Eudora Welty frequently uses first person passive narration to great effect because of her ear for southern dialect, and she has great fun doing it. In her novel, *The Ponder Heart*, narrator Edna Earle Ponder advises the reader, "And listen, if you read, you'll put your eyes out. Let's just talk." While the story that Edna Earle has to tell doesn't amount to much, listening to her tell it as a narrator is a pleasure.

The passive first person narrator usually is used to establish a *particular, circumscribed perspective*, or to create *immediacy or intensity*. But it can also *establish distance*, depending upon what the narrator himself sees and knows. That's the reason Thomas Mann used Serenus Zeitblom to relate the novel *Dr. Faustus*. He says, "My diary of the period does not record exactly when I made the decision to interpose the medium of the friend between myself and my subject; in other words not to tell the life of Adrian Leverkauhn directly but to have it told, and therefore, not to write a novel but a biography with all its trappings.... Besides, this strategy was a bitter necessity in order to achieve a certain humorous leavening of the somber material and to make its horrors bearable to myself as well as to the reader. To make the demonic strain pass through an undemonic medium, to entrust a harmless and simple soul, well-meaning and timid, with the recital of the story, was in itself a comic idea....

"But above all, the interposition of the narrator made it possible to tell the story on a dual plane of time, to weave together the events of the writer as he writes with those he is recounting, so that the quivering of his hand is ambiguously and yet obviously explained both by the vibration of distant bomb hits and by his inner consternation."

3. *Third person, external.* Here, the stage manager is in the shadows. He never speaks in the first person. Yet, we know that the narration is in the voice of a character with a distinct personality.

For example, let's go back to Bernard Malamud's "The Jewbird." Here's a narrator with a personality. It brings another layer of color to the story. More importantly, it permits interpretation, perspective, and tone. The story is fundamentally a tragedy about those modern Jews who deny and destroy their heritage, an act which Malamud considers anti-Semitic. In the story, Jews kill the Jewbird. Told in so objective and starkly real a fashion, it would have been a tract, a sermon. Leavened with the humor of a third person narrator who reveals only what he observes, it remains emphatic, but now balanced and palatable.

The third person external narrator tells someone else's story as he observes it through *ordinary* senses. He must remain *consistent throughout.* He cannot be an external observer, relating what he *sees* and *hears* in chapters one through five, and suddenly in chapter six reveal the *thoughts* of the characters. That would create a second narrative voice, a second stage manager, fracturing narrative consistency and destroying the unity of the story. It's like having Rembrandt paint the top half of a portrait and Van Gogh the bottom. Although both are immortal artists, the result would be a curiosity at best, certainly not art.

4. *Third person, internal.* When the narrator speaks in the third person internal voice, he has an

additional advantage: he can examine and reveal the thoughts of a *single* character. That allows him an intense identity with the lead character, and solves the problem of viewpoint without a second thought. It's why *Gone With the Wind* is Scarlett O'Hara's story, not Rhett Butler's, or Melanie's or Ashley's. We know everything about Scarlett from her own thoughts—her pettiness, her vanity, her pride, and her courage, and it was Mitchell's tenacity in clinging to Scarlett's viewpoint throughout the book that makes her heroine one of the strongest and most thoroughly developed characters in literature.

Here's what H. G. Wells did through the third person internal narrator in his novel, *The History of Mr. Polly*:

And Mr. Polly sat on the style and hated the whole scheme of his life—which was at once excessive and inadequate as a solution. He hated Foxbourne, he hated Foxbourne High Street, he hated his shop and his wife and his neighbors—every blessed neighbor—and with indescribable bitterness he hated himself....

He thought of religion as the recital of more or less incomprehensible words that were hard to remember, and of the divinity as a limitless being having the nature of a school master and making infinite rules, known and unknown rules, that were always ruthlessly enforced, and with an infinite capacity for punishment and, most horrible of all to think of, limitless powers of espial....

...Deep in the being of Mr. Polly, deep in that darkness like a creature which had been beaten about the head and left for dead but still lives, crawled a persuasion that over and above the things that are jolly and "bits of all right," there was beauty, there was delight, that somewhere—magically inaccessible perhaps, but still somewhere, were pure and easy and joyous states of body and mind.

He would sneak out on moonless winter nights and stare up at the stars and afterwards find it difficult to tell his father where he had been.

Another value of the third person internal voice is that it limits the narrator's awareness. He doesn't know everything. He doesn't see everything. He lives in the body and mind of one character, and that is the extent of his knowledge.

Some writers have used a variation on this third person, internal approach: They've allowed their narrators to escape the lead character to flit around the landscape making various observations—"While Bern lay recovering in the hospital room thinking how lucky he'd been to survive, his girlfriend Amethyst went horseback riding with Archie. They rode through dry, pollinating grass, sneezing along the way..." In this variation, the narrator freely observes whatever, whoever, and wherever he wishes—but he cannot enter the minds of other characters, only that of the lead.

5. *Semi-omniscient and omniscient.* There's an inherent irrationality in the variation I just mentioned, and it's even more obvious in the concept of an omniscient narrator. It should not trouble the writer who seeks no more than to amuse, or the reader whose goal

is to be entertained. On the other hand, the serious writer might be uncomfortable with an omniscient narrator who is restricted by no logical framework. If he pops into Mary's mind to examine her thoughts concerning John's motive, why does the narrator not simply pop into John's mind, discover the truth, and relieve the reader of suspense on page 3 rather than 303? Why this story instead of others which the narrator in his omniscience knows? The answer has to be arbitrary rather than rational, since the internal structure provides no limiting framework. For that reason, omniscience can be very difficult to handle successfully.

Yet, when the novice begins to write fiction, unless he has done some serious studying of the genre, he'll likely turn to an omniscient stage manager to tell his tale. That's because, first, he assumes that he himself is doing the narrating, which, I repeat, is *never* the case. Since he as writer knows everything, he takes for granted that his narrator must. Furthermore, an omniscient narrator *seems* to make things easier. The writer can *tell* the reader every last detail. But therein lies the trap.

I've just finished reading a potentially wonderful short story called, "The Day Mr. Devil Died." It was written by Mr. James Peel, a retired teacher living in Allentown, Pennsylvania. It has a pleasant, satisfying plot and perhaps the most careful rendering of a northern Louisiana dialect that I've ever read. But we are *told* that the women carried colorful plastic dime store sponges in their bodices with which to blot the sweat from their faces—a fact that only God and the women themselves can know—when we should simply observe the ladies taking the sponges from their bodices and touching them to their foreheads. Omniscience allows us to know *everything*, and when we know, there is the ever-present temptation to tell—and tell and tell, rather than to observe—and to observe only what we might reasonably see. There's no logical, internally justifiable reason for restraint in omniscient narrative. The decisions must be made arbitrarily, and the writer must exercise extraordinary self-discipline in not crossing the ethereal boundaries which he has arbitrarily set on his omniscience.

As Francis L. Fugate puts it in his book on viewpoint, "The omniscient viewpoint is one that is used by writers before they know any better. It was used considerably in Victorian vintage fiction, but fiction writing has come a long way since the quill pen era."

6. *The writer's "own" voice.* Finally, there is what many writers consider their own natural voice—or style—but I want to stress again (and I'll discuss this in detail in chapter five) that if this idea of a style is taken too literally, it becomes a lie. The simplest individual is complex, and the writer is highly complex and speaks with *many* natural voices, although he may prefer and hone and popularize just one. Here are three examples. You may recognize them by their content, but they're also easily identified through the unique voices of their creators:

I.

It was a pity to be obliged to reinvestigate the certitude of the moment itself and repeat how it had come to me as a revelation that the inconceivable communion I then surprised was a matter, for either party, of habit. It was a pity that I should have had to quaver out again the reasons for my not having, in my delusion, so much as questioned that the little girl saw our visitant even as I actually saw Mrs. Grose herself, and that she wanted, by just so much as she did thus see, to make me suppose she didn't, and at the same time, without showing anything arrive at a guess as to whether I myself did!

II.

No weather will be found in this book. This is an attempt to pull a book through without weather. It being the first attempt of the kind in fictitious literature, it may prove a failure, but it seemed worth the while of some dare-devil person to try it, and the author was in just the mood.

Many a reader who wanted to read a tale through was not able to do it because of delays on account of the weather. Nothing breaks up an author's progress like having to stop every few pages to fuss-up the weather. Thus it is plain that persistent intrusions of weather are bad for both reader and author.

Of course weather is necessary to a narrative of human experience. That is conceded. But it ought to be put where it will not be in the way; where it will not interrupt the flow of the narrative. And it ought to be the ablest weather that can be had, not ignorant, poor-quality, amateur weather. Weather is a literary specialty, and no untrained hand can turn out a good article of it. The present author can only do a few trifling ordinary kinds of weather, and he cannot do those very good. So it has seemed wisest to borrow such weather as is necessary for the book from qualified and recognized experts—giving credit, of course. This weather will be found over in the back of the book, out of the way. See Appendix. The reader is requested to turn over and help himself from time to time as he goes along.

III.

And now before me is a dreamy meadowland with a good old corral gate and a barbed wire fence the road running right on left but this where I get off at last. Then I crawl through the barbed wire and find myself trudging a sweet little sand road winding right thru fragrant dry heathers as tho I'd just popped thru from hell into familiar old Heaven on Earth, yair and Thank God (tho a minute later my heart's in my mouth again because I see black things in the white sand ahead but it's only piles of good old mule dung in Heaven).

I chose these examples because they're particularly representative of their creators. Even if you don't recognize the quotations from their sources, you have a fairly good chance of guessing their authors because of what you know about them as people.

Number I is difficult to read. It would earn a failing grade in any freshman composition course because the writer sacrifices clarity and conciseness of expression in order to impress us with his erudition. Never in the history of the world has a human being spoken this way, with the possible exception of Henry James. He was the ultimate intellectual. We know because he told us so repeatedly. He created some great literature, but worked hard to make clear that he was all intellect. He is easily identifiable in this passage from *The Turn of the Screw.*

Excerpt II is the voice of a born entertainer and communicator. The sentences are clear and to the point. The concept is comedic. It's what we expect from the personality of Samuel Clemens, and it appears in the introduction of his novel, *The American Claimant.*

In selection III, we find a narrator of free spirit, lacking in the discipline of accurate spelling and sentence structure. Just as he is physically wandering through a "dreamy meadowland," his writing style wanders, lazy and unfettered. The writer, we might guess, is a vagabond of sorts. And we'd be correct, for he's Jack Kerouac, author of several books that capture the spirit of the 1950's beat/hippie movement, including *The Dharma Bums,* from which this is taken.

These are examples of the writer's natural voice—his style. Most beginning writers feel like logs adrift at sea, yearning for the anchor of their own personal styles. Experts talk about it, write about it, read about it, but—there's *nothing to it.* (I'm speaking from the writer's perspective, not the reader's.) Style in everyday life is who you are; *style in writing is who you are on paper.* Style begins and ends with who you are.

"Young writers often suppose that style is a garnish for the meat of prose," write Strunk and White, "a sauce by which a dull dish is made palatable. Style has no such separate entity; it is non-detachable, unfilterable. The beginner should approach style warily, realizing that it is himself he is approaching, no other; and he should begin by turning resolutely away from all devices that are popularly believed to indicate style—all mannerisms, tricks, adornments. The approach to style is by way of plainness, simplicity, orderliness, sincerity."

I have never found an exception to this observation: Timid people write timidly; passionate people write passionately, with power. If I can read what you've written I can tell what sort of person you are. If I know who you are, I can tell how you'll write. You can't put on paper what's not inside you.

Tennessee Williams felt that "the power of a writer is very closely related to sexuality, sexual power." Lady Mary Wortley-Montagu said the same of Henry Fielding, although more euphemistically: "I am sorry for H. Fielding's death, not only as I shall read no more of his writings, but I believe he lost more than others, as no man enjoyed life more than he did, though few had less reason to do so, the highest of his preferment being raking in the lowest sinks of vice and misery. ...His happy constitution (even when he had, with great pains, half demolished it) made him forget everything when he was before a venison pasty, or over a flask of champagne; and I am persuaded that he has known more happy moments than any prince upon earth."

E. M. Forster dismisses Sir Walter Scott by urging us to "think how all Scott's laborious mountains and scooped-out glens and carefully ruined abbeys call out for passion, passion, and how it is never there! If he had passion he would be a great writer.... But he only has a temperate heart and gentlemanly feelings and an intelligent affection for the country-side: and this is not basis enough for great novels."

No one puts it better than Somerset Maugham in his *The Art of Fiction*. After describing what he believes are among the ten best novels in the English language, he concludes that the authors were one and all persons of marked and unusual individuality. "They had a passion for writing and a creative instinct. But the quality that pulls it all together," says Maugham, "is *personality*. Yes, the literary artist needs intelligence, but of a peculiar and perhaps not a very high order, and these great writers were intelligent; but they were not strikingly intellectual. And there is on occasion inspiration."

What set these writers apart was the passion of their personalities. Says Maugham, "On the whole, these great writers, with the exception of Emily Bronte and Dostoyevsky, must have been very pleasant to meet. They had vitality, they were good company and great talkers, and their charm impressed everyone who came in contact with them. They had a prodigious power of enjoyment, and loved the good things of life.... There is an exuberance in his [the writer's] nature that leads him to display."

Writers can't help expressing who they are—art always reflects the heart and soul of its maker. In his greatest works, Michelangelo confessed in silent, plaintive honesty his love for male beauty; Van Gogh virtually wept in hunger for sunlight; Raphael lusted for the soft, robust pulchritude of women.

Writing style is being who you are on paper. That's what great writers mean when they talk of honesty, simplicity and an absence of pretentiousness. Emily Dickinson was as passionate as D. H. Lawrence. She expressed herself more circumspectly and more delicately. But the passion is still there, still obvious.

That's who Emily Dickinson *was*. That's her *style*, the expression of who she was on paper. Stendhal was impulsive, impetuous, and that's a key to his style. According to Andre Gide, "The great secret of Stendhal, his great shrewdness, consisted in writing *at once*. His thought charged with emotion remains as lively, as fresh in colour as the newly developed butterfly that the collector has surprised as it was coming out of the cocoon. Whence that element of alertness and spontaneity, of incongruity, of suddenness and nakedness, that always delights us anew in his style? It would seem that his thought does not take time to put on its shoes before beginning to run."

Stendhal himself described a book he'd read, in which the writing exaggerated the thoughts and feelings, as being horribly turgid. "This fault is the worst of all in my view," he said; "it is the one that most blunts the sensibility. One should not write unless one has important and profoundly beautiful things to say, but then one must say them with the utmost simplicity, as though one were trying to get them by unnoticed. This is the opposite of what all the fools of this century do, but it is what all great men accomplish."

Thomas Hardy declared that the secret of a living style "lies in not having too much style. Being in fact a little careless, or rather seeming to be, here and there." This naturalness, which, in effect, is being one's self, "brings wonderful life into writing."

Artists who understood passions wrote of them honestly. They didn't try to be original or subtle, but, being unique and complex personalities, their honest work turned out to be original and subtle. With the exception of Flaubert, they didn't seek to be great stylists. They wrote simply and straight-forwardly in what they might have considered their natural voices.

But don't make the mistake of thinking any writer writes in what is truly his natural voice—and for goodness sake, don't waste good time trying to find yours. In fact, every competent writer has a *host* of styles; Somerset Maugham, who wrote many books including *Of Human Bondage*, said, "Every novel demands its own particular style..."

And even within the same book a writer's voice shifts as he speaks as various characters—young and old, beautiful and homely, self-doubting and confident. How can this be done? By taking notes of what we observe in the world around us, as some writing teachers urge? While note-taking isn't likely to do much harm, it certainly isn't the key to the many voices of the literary artist. The primary source of understanding others, of creating characters, is understanding ourselves. Emerson knew what he was talking about when he said, "To understand in your heart that what is true for you is true for all mankind—that is genius." Saul Bellow is Hertzog—and all the others. Margaret Mitchell is Scarlett—and Melanie and Ashley, and a somewhat less successful Rhett. It's called acting, and we'll get back to it in chapter five, but first we must see about set design.

CHAPTER IV
Description

A student in an article writing course I taught a few years ago, a bright young man in his mid-twenties, began a query letter with an anecdote. Usually, that's a good idea—it catches the editor's interest while also introducing the subject of the proposal. Unfortunately, it didn't work in this case. That's because the anecdote took up the first page of a two-page letter.

"I don't know how much to describe!" the student confessed.

"How much description is enough?" I'm asked frequently. Let me answer it by returning to our metaphor: Literary art exists in the theater of the reader's imagination.

Now, if you're staging a play, unless you're doing something experimental, you'll want at least some furnishings, a few props, and a backdrop. The same is true of good story writing—but there's a difference, and it's an exciting one: The writer doesn't want to complete the set, but merely to sketch it. Why? For the same reason that people often prefer the book to the movie. They don't want to be *told* everything. They want to *participate* in the co-creative process. That is why serious readers read rather than watch TV. They, too, want to exercise their imaginations. It's a truth not sufficiently recognized and respected by writers themselves.

Yet, suppose I tell you that a woman stood on a street corner wearing a form-fitting red dress and matching high heels with a cigarette between her fingers. Would you have any trouble envisioning her? In fact, you've already filled in all sorts of details. My guess is that you've made her a blonde, and you've painted her lips bright red. Or, perhaps you've given her red hair—if it doesn't matter to the story line, why should the writer deprive you of the pleasure of co-creativity by insisting that she's a blonde?

But the reader can only contribute so much, and knowing those limitations helps the writer to decide how much description is necessary. The reader is limited by 1) his experience, 2) his imagination, and 3) his patience.

The Reader's Experience

For example, I'm not saying much if I write that a curtain is a magenta satin and the reader doesn't know what magenta means. In that case, words work *against* my creative intent. The reader is torn from his imaginative experience to consciousness of the word itself. The set—which is all the description that locates the story in time and space—must relate to the reader's experience if he's to construct it in his imagination. That doesn't mean that the reader must know *every* word the writer uses; on the contrary, one benefit of reading is to enlarge the vocabulary. But the writer must be sensitive to the possibility that he might be going beyond his readers' experience and make sure that the context clarifies his meaning or makes the details unimportant.

Joyce's *Ulysses* is an excellent example of an effort failing to speak to the reader's experience. Here's how Joyce himself translated a single paragraph of his book to Harriet Shaw Weaver; first, the paragraph: "Unslow, malswift, pro mean, proh noblesse, Atrahora, Melancolores, nears; whos glaque eyes glitt bedimmd to imm! whose fingrings creep o'er skull: till, qwench! asterr mist calls estarr and grauw! honath John raves homes glowcoma."

With some luck you might guess correctly the meaning of Melancolores (melancholy), glitt (insight), mist calls, raves, homes and glowcoma (glaucoma). Much of the rest is beyond hope. According to Joyce, Unslow does not mean "not slow," but inevitably. Atrahora is from the Latin and means black hour; asterr (Greek) is star, and estarr (German) is blindness. This sort of thing simply is not literature. It's a brilliantly conceived language puzzle, and, although *Ulysses* contains passages of the highest literary achievement, nothing is gained by playing the part of the sheep-like masses of "The Emperor's New Clothes." *One function of literature is to communicate*, and that must take place within the framework of the reader's experience.

The Reader's Imagination

That doesn't mean that the written description must be a literal counterpart to the reader's experience. Just as readers can use the context of an unknown word and their own imaginations to arrive at an adequate definition, they can also use their imaginations to bridge the gap between experience and the writer's descriptions. That's what the co-creativity between writer and reader is all about. But, for the process to succeed, the writer must build upon universally shared experiences.

Anne Rice does so skillfully in *Interview With a Vampire*. None of us understands firsthand the vampire's thirst for blood. We lack experience. So Rice has a vampire put it in terms we *do* understand:

"For I guarantee you that if you walk the streets tonight and strike down a woman as rich and beautiful as Babette and suck her blood until she drops at your feet you will have no hunger left for Babette's profile in the candlelight or for listening by the window for the sound of her voice. You will be filled, Louis, as you were meant to be, with all the life that you can hold; and you will have hunger when that's gone for the same and the same, and the same..."

Here is lust fulfilled. We can understand that. And here is power: "...you will see death in all its beauty, life as it is only known on the very point of death.... You...alone...under the rising moon...can strike like the hand of God!"

The writer's responsibility is to give the reader something for his imagination to build upon. How much he must give depends upon the background and experience of his intended readers.

Here's another example:

"Stephen preached to the multitudes saying, 'You stiff-necked and uncircumcised of heart and ear, you have always resisted the Holy Spirit, you the same as your fathers! Which of the prophets have not your fathers persecuted?...'

"As they heard this they were enraged at heart and gnashed their teeth at him; but he, full of the Holy Spirit, looked up into heaven and saw the glory of God and Jesus standing at God's right hand, and said, 'I see the heavens opened and the Son of Man standing at God's right hand.'

"But they, shouting loudly and holding their hands to their ears, rushed upon him in a body and, dragging him out of the city, they stoned him. And the witnesses placed their clothes at the feet of a young man named Saul." (Acts 7:51-58, Berkeley version)

How are we able to envision that scene when the author has given us no description, placed no furniture whatever on the stage for us? Through the co-creativity of reader and writer. At some point in our experience, we've met Stephen. He's young and passionate, intelligent, believing, and naive. His hair is blonde and he is blue-eyed and wearing a brown robe. Or—he's a former skeptic, just recently converted. He speaks not from optimism but bitterness. His hair is black, contrasting with the flowing white robe. Although not one of us may envision the same Stephen, we are all clear about what he looks like through our imaginations.

The Reader's Patience

People shouldn't have to read essays to understand a painting, or take a college course to appreciate a novel. The best writers are not demanding of the reader. They're not selfish. No matter how seriously they take their art, they understand that the reader has paid for his seat and deserves a satisfying show, not a tedious test of endurance.

We've all read descriptions that are too rich, too detailed, too boringly verbose. Even great writers, more commonly in earlier centuries but not rarely today, get caught up in painting unnecessarily elaborate backdrops and cluttering the stage with unneeded furniture. Henry James recognized and admonished against it in his own verbose fashion, but no one has made that point more effectively than Willa Cather: "The novel for a long while has been over-furnished. The property-man has been so busy on its pages, the importance of material objects and their vivid presentation have been so stressed, that we take it for granted that whoever can observe and can write the English language can write a novel...."

Cather questions whether such detailed description has any place in imaginative art, and specifically criticizes Balzac, saying, "To reproduce on paper the actual city of Paris; the houses, the upholstery, the food, the wines, the game of pleasure, the game of business, the game of finance: a stupendous ambition but after all, unworthy of an artist."

The serious writer doesn't produce a snapshot of life. The snapshot includes everything, and the *everything* distracts from the *specific something* to be examined. Literature, whether fact or fiction, isn't a photographic depiction of reality but the *simplification* and *clarification* of one aspect of reality, the airbrushing out of background detail, the darkening into shadows of real-life clutter and distraction, in order to intensify that which is to be focused upon. The criterion for including material—background, furnishings, props— isn't that they're "true," or interesting, but that they *contribute* to the creative intent.

Cather concludes, "How wonderful it would be if we could throw all of the furniture out of the window; and along with it all the meaningless reiterations concerning physical sensations, all the tiresome old patterns, and leave the room as bare as the stage of a Greek theater, or as the house into which the glory of Pentecost descended; leave the scene bare for the play of emotions, great and little—for the nursery tale, no less than the tragedy, is killed by tasteless amplitude. The elder Dumas enunciated a great principle when he said that to make a drama, a man needed one passion, and four walls."

The writer must ask himself: *Is this description necessary?* If the answer is yes, then, *how much of this description is necessary?* One needn't describe in page after page a young man's determination to break into the upper crust of society, certain that he can do it and committed through faith to the proposition that it is worth doing. It's enough to say, as Fitzgerald does in *The Great Gatsby*:

"If personality is an unbroken series of successful gestures, then there was something gorgeous about him, some heightened sensitivity to the promises of life, as if he were related to one of those intricate machines that register earthquakes ten thousand miles away...it was an extraordinary gift for hope, a romantic readiness such as I have never found in any other person and which it is not likely I shall ever find again."

Entire books have been performed on sparsely furnished stages. How much did Hemingway tell us about the fisherman in *The Old Man in the Sea*? What did Hawthorne have to say about Hester Prynne's environment? We're told very little about the lead characters of many modern short stories—yet, we feel that we know them well. A good example is Sammy in John Updike's short story "A & P." Upon a second reading, we're surprised to discover how little of our image of Sammy came from Updike. Most of it comes from us.

Each reader brings his own vision, his own experience to what he reads, and the serious writer understands in humility that nothing he ever does is finished by himself, that he owes the completion of it to his readers. And those readers want to share in the co-creative process.

The human personality is creative, and most people, regardless of their social position, hunger to express themselves creatively. Mass entertainment provides little opportunity for co-creativity. Everything comes *at* us, all explained and described, while we passively observe. The best writing offers an alternative. It requires us to join in, to exercise our natural gift of imagination.

The finest writers understand this. According to Chekhov, "Descriptions of nature should be very brief and have an incidental character. Commonplaces like: 'the setting sun bathing in the waves of the darkening sea, flooded with purple and gold,' etc...should be finished with." The reader can supply that detail—and wants to. All he needs is the right hint from the writer, and Chekhov points the way to that: "In descriptions of Nature one has to snatch at small details, grouping them in such a manner that after reading them one can obtain the picture on closing one's eyes.

"For instance you will get a moonlight night if you write that on the dam of the mill a fragment of broken bottle flashed like a small bright star, and there rolled by, like a ball, the black shadow of a dog or a wolf—and so on."

Here are two fine examples of description, both published in James White's book *Clarity*. The first, from "The Nightingales Sing," is by Elizabeth Persons (the italics are mine):

"Joanna let herself in the front door and turned to wave to Phil, who waved back and drove off down the *leafy* street, *misty* in the *midnight silence.* Inland, the fog was not as bad as it had been near the sea, but the trees *dripped with the wetness* and the *sidewalk shone* under the street light. She listened to the faraway, *sucking sound* of Phil's tires die away; then she sighed and closed the door and moved sleepily into the *still house, dropping her key into the brass bowl* on the hall table. The house was cool, and *dark* downstairs except for *the hall light,* and it *smelled of the earth* in her mother's little conservatory."

The reader needs this information. For one thing it sets the precise mood that Persons is after. You need to know that the trees dripped with wetness and the sidewalks shone under the street light. The reader can use his own imagination to build on those vivid details. One word, *still,* (she moved sleepily into the still house), heightens our senses and when she drops her key into the brass bowl on the hall table, we're quite jolted by the loudness of the clank *although it is never mentioned*!

The second example is from William Goyen's "The Grasshopper's Burden":

"Here was this school building in the town, holding young and old, this stone building that looked from the front like a great big head with flat skull of asphalt and gravel and face of an insect that might be eating up the young through its opening and closing mouth of doors; and across its forehead were written the words: 'Dedicated to all high enterprise, the building of good citizens of the world, the establishment of a community of minds and hearts, free men and women.'"

This is all that need be said about the building. We know it's ugly, intimidating, impersonal. The hook the reader needs for his own co-creativity is the mood that the building evokes, and Goyen gives us that clearly and concisely.

Selecting just a few effective props and furnishings requires acuity of the writer's senses—alertness to specific, sensuous, representative *detail* and not the broad, general, and hackneyed. And where do we get that evocative detail? From our own lives, the everyday lives that seem so trivial by virtue of our living them. The Prince of Wales undoubtedly considers the business of princing a bore. But if we don't find the clanking pots in our own experience, we won't find them at all.

"The stories were awful," says Eudora Welty of her early efforts. "I am from Jackson, Mississippi, and never had been much of anywhere else, but the action in my stories took place in Paris.... When I wrote the stories about Paris I thought I was very good. I think that you are likely to believe that something you write is good so long as it is about something of which you are totally ignorant.... Then I went home and started writing about what I knew. I was older and I guess I had a little more sense, enough sense so that I could see the great rift between what I wrote and what was the real thing."

Until now, we've been discussing props and furnishings, but there's more to designing the set, and it's critical: the story's *backdrop*—its environment or atmosphere or location. As R. V. Cassill explains in *Writing Fiction*: "The way the objective world is depicted hints at the mood of the people who inhabit it. A crude illustration of this can be given by saying that a description of night, fog and cold will hint that the characters are miserable or depressed. Descriptions of meadows in May will hint at some level of happiness." He adds, "a virtuoso performance in using the altering aspects of the exterior world to show the alterations of the psyche is Thomas Mann's *Death in Venice*. There the city in various weathers becomes 'mirror and image' of the subconscious changes in the main character."

Robert Lewis Stevenson was particularly sensitive to the unifying value of a story's environment. He wrote:

"...tracts of young fir, and low rocks that reach into deep soundings particularly torture and delight me. Something must have happened in such places, and perhaps ages back, to members of my race; and when I was a child I tried in vain to invent appropriate games for them and I still try, just as vainly, to fit them with the proper story. Some places speak distinctly. Certain dank gardens cry aloud for a murder; certain old houses demand to be haunted; certain coasts are set apart for shipwrecks....

"In this way, the setting may, in many cases, exist as the initial element of the narrative, and suggest an action appropriate to itself."

Unlike the fiction writer, the writer of fact obviously can't create an ideal environment for his story, but he can *comment* on what he gets stuck with if he has chosen an accommodating narrator to tell his story. For example, if a tragic funeral takes place on a sunny day, he has every right to say that the day should have been overcast, or cold and drizzly. He can also select detail—a teary-eyed child, a dead leaf, a lonely, empty expanse of ground. But he's limited by truth.

The fiction writer, on the other hand, has no excuse for not making the best possible use of environment. Eudora Welty, who is a very visual writer, explains why she chose the settings she did in two of her novels: "It was a matter of setting the stage and confining the story. These are both family stories and I didn't want them inhibited by outward events I couldn't control. In the case of *Delta Wedding*, I remember I made a careful investigation to find a year in which nothing very terrible had happened in the Delta by way of floods or fires or wars which would have taken them away.... In the case of *Losing Battles*, I wanted to write about a family who had *nothing*. A bare stage. I chose the time that was the very hardest, when people had the least, so that the stage could be the barest and that was the Depression, of course...."

Watch how the backdrop comes to life in Katherine Mansfield's story "At The Bay":

"A heavy dew had fallen. The grass was blue. Big drops hung on the bushes and just did not fall; the silvery, fluffy toi-toi was limp on its long stalks, and all the marigolds and the pinks in the bungalow gardens were bowed to the earth with wetness. Drenched were the cold fuchsias, round pearls of dew lay on the flat nasturtium leaves. It looked as though the sea had beaten up softly in the darkness, as though one immense wave had come rippling—how far? Perhaps if you had wakened up in the middle of the night you may have seen a big fish flicking in at the window and gone again....

"Ah-aah! sounded the sleepy sea. And from the bush there came the sound of little streams flowing, quickly, lightly, slipping between the smooth stones, gushing into ferny basins and out again; and there was the splashing of big drops on large leaves, and something else—what was it!—a faint stirring and shaking, the snapping of a twig and then such silence that it seemed someone was listening."

Occasionally, the setting—the environment and atmosphere—does more than reflect the theme and intent of the story. In some cases it takes on personality, becomes a character, even a leading character. Thomas Hardy, for example, did not devote the first five pages of *The Return of the Native* to a description of Egdon Heath naively. He did so to set the tone and character of the entire book through the "personality" of the heath:

> The sombre stretch of rounds and hollows seemed to rise and meet the evening gloom in pure sympathy, the heath exhaling darkness as rapidly as the heavens precipitated it. And so the obscurity in the air and the obscurity in the land closed together in a black fraternization towards which each advanced halfway.
>
> The place became full of a watchful intentness; for when other things sank brooding to sleep the heath appeared slowly to awake and listen. Every night its Titanic form seemed to await something; but it had waited thus unmoved, during so many centuries, through the crises of so many things that it could only be imagined to await one last crisis—the final overthrow....

[A] sort of intensity was often arrived at during winter darkness, tempests, and mists. Then Egdon was aroused to reciprocity; for the storm was its lover and the wind its friend. Then it became the home of strange phantoms; and it was found to be the hitherto unrecognized original of those wild regions of obscurity which are vaguely felt to be compassing about in midnight dreams of flight and disaster, and are never thought of after the dream till revived by scenes like this.

A story's environment isn't selected as a casual afterthought. It really *does* matter in terms of overall unifying effect whether the sun is shining or the sky is overcast, whether the forest is of tall, dense pine or scrawny saplings rising from a charred floor. In the best writing, the environment is integral to the creative intent of the work, and the fortunate writer receives the entire package whole. Most work at it, understanding that the setting must *contribute* to the overall effect. It isn't enough that it not detract.

But another paradox: Some settings have become clichés and are no longer an option to the sensitive writer. Stevenson's houses made to be haunted have been exorcised by overuse, and it's to author J. Anson's credit, or that of the spooks involved, that the house of *The Amityville Horror* was modern, not Gothic or Victorian.

In literature, murders now have a much harder time getting committed during violent thunderstorms. Lovers avoid pastures of clover, and people resist romance over candlelit cocktail tables. It has all become too common, too trite. Such environments have lost their freshness because they *are* so effective, and today's writer was born too late. If he uses these clichés at all, he must find new ways to bring them to life. Better still, he should leave them to the writers of mass market romances, and do the hard work of creating freshly evocative settings for future generations of writers to make hackneyed.

To summarize, then: The writer needs to provide setting, props, and backdrop, but the most effective techniques are those that include the reader in the creative process. That means providing all that's necessary as a foothold for the reader's imagination, and allowing her to take it from there. Every writer will answer the question, "How much is necessary?" differently. That's what makes each artist's work unique.

CHAPTER V
The Writer as Actor

Many years ago, I walked along Broadway with Flora Rita Schreiber, author of *Sibyl* and *The Shoemaker*. We'd been to the monthly meeting of the American Society of Journalists and Authors, and it was near midnight as we entered the theater district. In a handful of months, Flora had gone from a hard working college instructor and part-time writer to an international author and talk show celebrity.

"How are you handling all the pressure?" I asked.

"Oh, I love it!" she responded, and literally pirouetted on the sidewalk. Then, throwing her arms wide, she said, "All my life I've wanted to be a performer, and now at last I've made it." Indeed she had, and in ways very few would ever know.

In *Sibyl,* Flora starred as a host of people—most of Sibyl's sixteen multiple personalities. And she told me when I interviewed her some time later for a *TV Guide* article, that these personalities were not as distinct in reality as she had to make them for the reader. In a sense, she created these people, then played each role to perfection on the pages of her book.

The writer is an actor. As I've said earlier, many are actually drawn to the stage, in addition to the printed word. And even if they don't get before a live audience, most professionals recognize the theatrical nature of their business. If you can think of your writing as acting in print, you will discover for yourself how dramatically that awareness can simplify the writer's task.

I'll be referring to my own writing a good deal in this chapter, primarily because I'm the only writer whose motives I completely understand. What's more, I've had a career that has spanned a great deal more territory than is usual. That's because I decided as a teenager that life was too short to work for a living—and by work I meant doing the same repetitive activity days, months, and years on end. I didn't mind in the least putting out a prodigious effort as long as I would not be bored. My first professional work as a writer was with Rodale Press, the health and fitness publishing company. For five years, I wrote about vitamins, minerals, fibers, jogging, and positive thinking. I traveled all over the country, interviewed celebrities, politicians, and scientists, did investigative pieces, and had such fun that for three years I forgot to take vacations. Then the work became routine, and after three more years I quit to escape the boredom. A year later I accepted an offer to return to the company for twice the salary I had been making—because I was poor. Two years later I quit for good because I was bored, and preferred poverty to boredom.

From then on, although I still wrote about health, fitness, and medicine on occasion, I specialized in being a generalist. That is, I researched and wrote about subjects of interest to me, issues I considered important. Luckily, I've been blessed with an enormous curiosity and enthusiasm for life, and I still have more ideas in my files than I could pursue in two lifetimes. I've made a living writing on a virtual encyclopedia of subjects.

Here's the point: In writing both fiction and fact for children, mechanics, physicians, male college students, housewives, business women, the elderly, educators, and scientists, *I've played each of those roles in the theater of my readers' imaginations.*

It would have been impossible to write in so many styles. Here's how this works. A few years ago, *Boys' Life* editor William Morris asked me to do a piece on anabolic steroids, the drugs athletes illegally take to build muscle. No snap assignment, this. A large percentage of *Boys' Life* readers are twelve and thirteen years old. They're going to be bored silly by a technical article on anabolic something-or-other.

How do I know that—because I'm a veteran fifty-year-old writer? Not at all. I know that because, for this assignment, I'm a really brilliant thirteen-year-old boy.

Now I know what's fun—and what's hopelessly dull. *Now* I know what words I understand, and the ones I don't. I know the sort of lead that will catch my attention, and which ones will get me to turn the page at a snap. And so I write:

"I'm one happy dude!"

Countless millions of TV viewers saw the smile on Jeff Blatnick's sweat-drenched face when he said those words. They saw the tears in his eyes, too, It was another Jeff Blatnick miracle.

The first was at age 15, when he survived a plane crash.

Then, two years ago, doctors told him he had cancer. Jeff underwent surgery and radiation therapy—and survived.

And now this. Beneath the blazing lights of Los Angeles Coliseum, while thousands cheered, Jeff pulled a last minute upset to win America's first ever Olympic medal in Greco-Roman wrestling—super heavyweight division.

It was the gold.

The odds were against Jeff at the Olympics, too. The American magazine *Sports Illustrated* gave him an outside chance to take third place and a bronze medal.

On the mat that night, Jeff faced Thomas Johansson of Sweden. Johansson was heavier, 270 pounds to Jeff's 240. Weight means a lot in Greco-Roman wrestling. Since you can't hold your opponent below the waist—no tackling his legs to get him on the canvas—you must use your weight, strength and leverage to throw him off balance.

Get him off his feet and you've scored one point. Force him to his stomach and it's worth two. If you roll him to his back, that's three points.

Johansson had another advantage, too, although no one but Johansoon knew about it at the time. He'd been taking illegal drugs, called steroids, to make himself stronger.

That *Boys' Life* article, "They Won Without Steroids," proved to be one of the most popular of the year. I hope it helped some boys to avoid the dangers of steroid abuse. (It was at the time that Lyle Alzado was dying of brain cancer and blaming it on anabolic steroids.) I could never have written it as Robert Bahr.

For an article on antique motorcycles, I needed a much different character to write:

Charles George of Quakertown, PA has a little good luck and a lot of common sense. A few months ago he came across a 1925 Indian Chief motorcycle with a Princess sidecar. The bike was complete and original, but a beaten-up mess. So Charlie gave it a total restoration, then advertised it in *Hemmings Motor News* and sold it—to film star Steve McQueen, as it turned out.

In nearby Boyertown, Bill Patt was driving past an apple orchard and spotted a 1929 Indian Scout, fenders deep in mud. "It must have been there for 20 years— maybe 30," says Bill. "The tires were completely rotted."

The engine was missing, along with the gas tank and transmission, but Bill discovered them in the trunk of a dilapidated car nearby. He found the farmer, offered $25.00 for the whole heap and took it home. Today that cycle, nearly 50 years old, runs like a top, a mechanical wonder that wins trophies annually without fail as an unrestored antique.

Popular Mechanics bought that piece. To write it, I took on a personality as different from the real me as I can imagine: an overweight mechanically-oriented jock who drinks beer, loves football and describes himself as a good ol' boy.

As a physicist, I wrote for *Biomedical News,* "A mathematical model of airflow rate in deep sea divers, which makes it possible for the first time to predict the quantity of oxygen consumed to carry on the work of breathing at various depths up to 1,000 feet, has been developed by two Temple University researchers."

As a businessman, I wrote for the President's Council on Physical Fitness and Sports: "The cost of physical degeneration is high for American industry. Roy J. Shephard, M.D., Ph.D., of the University of Toronto's Department of Physiological Hygiene, writes in the June issue of *The Archives of Environmental Health:* 'The economic costs of chronic cardiovascular disease are staggering.'"

As a grandfather, a quarter of a century older than Robert Bahr, I pulled up a lawn chair and wrote for *Mature Health:*

> I'm reminded of the starlings that nested in the eaves of our porch last spring. They were noisy critters, those newborn birds, gulping down anything their harried parents dropped into their gaping beaks. And what a delightful life those young ones had—eating, sleeping, no responsibilities.
>
> But apparently it wasn't all that it was cracked up to be, because the day came when three of those four youngsters flapped their wings a few times and, with some foolhardy obsession, hurled them-

selves from the nest. They plummeted to within a hair's breadth of the concrete porch, then swooped up and out through the branches of trees, the stretch of grass, the pond, and settled triumphantly on the limb of a pine to overlook the vastness of the world through their own eyes. Only the lone straggler sat in the nest, still chirping to be fed.

But not for long. A few days later I watched as the mother bird nudged him—gently at first, and then more force-fully, coaxing that timid fellow to get out as he was meant to do, to live his own life. And finally he did, soaring off as skillful-ly as the others, flying as high in spite of his reticence.

It seemed a pretty easy thing for that Momma bird to do (or perhaps it was a Poppa bird, I'm no authority on such things). Perhaps birds are more in touch with biological reality.

As I said, I'm no expert. But I believe that it hurts them as much as it does us to send off their young. Momma and Poppa birds simply respond to an instinctual awareness that if the young are to survive and flourish they must set off on their own.

I've been a woman. I've been a very young child. I've been a fundamentalist pervert. But my most satis-fying role was that of God, a position thrust upon me by the requirements of the opening chapter of my fact book *The Blizzard.* Although two weeks of painstaking research went into writing those few pages, they had a sweeping, fictional quality intended to set them apart from the human struggles which made up the bulk of the book:

In the autumn each year, the sun remains low on the arctic horizon, its rays merely glancing across the north summit of the earth. Its heat there is lost into space; its illumination, distorted through greater distances of atmosphere, washes the ice in azure and pink, orange and vermillion. With shortening days, the sky grows deep blue, and even at midday stars glow in the far sky. Where the ice has not yet formed, the sea is black.

With dusk on November 24, 1976, two months of night settled upon the Arctic. Yet the darkness was relative, for the sky over much of that five and half million square miles of mostly frozen sea was clean and rare, and the stars in the north constellation cast brilliant reflections over the patches of water.

Moreover, a full moon appeared and drifted along the horizon for eighteen hours. Too low to illuminate the deep crags of the glaciers, those places remained in unbroken darkness. But it gleamed across all the desolate islands and sweeping treeless tundra, upon thousands of miles of surf breaking and freezing over rocky beaches. Across all the vast open space of the North—the floes, the plains of ice and dark patches of sea—the moonlight fell pure and cold. That night the sterile light swept the unbroken ice of the East Siberian Sea and the Greenland ice pack. Off the coast of Norway it made radiant the scaring cliffs of glacial ice. Near Svalbard Island, an ice floe reflected the moon's rays against the belly of a solitary cloud. Thus, two moons of almost equal intensity brightened the island.

Near Victoria Island in the Canadian archipelago, a light breeze swept millions of ice crystals into the air. In the moonlight, they glittered like the dust of diamonds, showering the desolate land with opalescence.

White bears stood motionless on the ice, casting shadows, while ringed seals lingered near their breathing holes in the floes, and giant walruses, resting nearby, lifted unblinking eyes to survey the night for approaching bears...

Across all the Arctic the temperature continued to drop. The upper air, now profoundly cold and heavy, began to spread like a great blanket over the surface of the earth. Layer upon layer it accumulated, thickening, bulging into an inverted bowl, finally growing into an enormous mountain of dense and sluggish air, its invisible crest towering many miles above Everest, piercing the belly of the stratosphere.

On November 25, 1976, the center of this great mass was at 80 degrees latitude, north of the Laptev Sea. But it spilled south in every direction—from northern Siberia almost to Greenland, from the tiny islands above Norway to the Bering Strait. Bubbles breaking from the mass drifted toward the Aleutian Islands, Alaska and northern Canada. In the United States, they reached as far south as Buffalo.

Yes, sometimes the writer must even assume the role of God. But the writer is an actor in more than his narrative—or stage manager—voice. He must also become each of his characters. In the writing of fact, he's most effective when he *becomes* the true-life people of his anecdotes and extended scenarios. He's limited, of course, by the truth, so that the fact writer does not invent the character, but becomes him or her through intense identification.

Sometimes that can become an almost eerie experience. In the late 1970's, I was writing *Least of All Saints*, the biography of Aimee Semple McPherson, for Prentice-Hall. I traced her life from her birth in Ontario, Canada, to the mission fields of China, then back to New York City after the death of her husband Robert Semple. I knew that in New York she had met her second husband, Harry, but I didn't know how. In order not to break the flow of the narrative, for my own purposes only, I invented a scene based on my complete identification with Aimee. I had her walk up to a young man, a complete stranger, start a conversation and offer him her newspaper. The following year, I learned that Harry was still alive in Titusville, Florida. I travelled there to interview him a few months before he died and discovered that it wasn't a newspaper but an umbrella she offered to share with him on a rainy day!

The writer is more frequently recognized as an actor in the creation of fictional characters. Mario Vargas Losa illustrates that in his novel *Aunt Julia and the Scriptwriter* when he has his Bolivian writer, Pedro Camacho, come to work each morning wearing a new costume—a tuxedo, a dress, depending upon which character he's to feature in his script that day.

George Simenon has said, "When I begin a novel I become its principal character, and my whole life from morning till night is conditioned by that character; I am really inside his skin. Before writing a novel, at the moment when I must enter what I call a state of grace, I must in fact empty myself of myself, empty everything that is my personality in order to become purely receptive, able to absorb other characters and other impressions."

Flaubert spoke of the same experience when he said, "Madame Bovary *is* me." Henry James was virtually obsessed with the woman he was later to write about in *Portrait of a Lady*, long before he had a story to put her in. "Thus I had my vivid individual," he said, "vivid, so strangely, in spite of being still at large, not confined by the conditions, not engaged in the tangle, to which we look for much of the empress that constitutes an identity."

It's no accident that Hermann Hesse began *Demian* with the words, "I cannot tell my story without reaching a long way back. If it were possible I would reach back farther still—into the very first years of my childhood, and beyond them into distant ancestral past.... this is my story; it is the story of a man, not of an invented, or possible, or idealized, or otherwise absent figure, but of a unique being of flesh and blood."

In fact, *Demian* is a novel, not an autobiography, but Hesse *became* his lead character nonetheless through his capacity as actor. There's something mystical about this assumption of another personality. It's what Dickens achieved and expressed in the first paragraph of *David Copperfield*: "Whether I shall turn out to be the hero by my own life, or whether that station will be held by anybody else, these pages must now show." It's probably why he wrote so often in the first person—he was one of the greater actors in the history of literature. A biographer, Amerongen, writes, "It is only natural that in these [Dickens'] readings, even more than in his play-acting, his extraordinary powers of assuming another character should have had the fullest scope." He continues: "Dickens' oldest daughter tells us that her father used to say that when, as a boy, he was reading his favorite novels, he would *be* Tom Jones or some sea-captain in the British Navy, a fact corroborated afterwards in *Copperfield*. Later on, his characters became such absolute realities to him that he fancied he met them in the streets, that he laughed and cried with them. He made himself ill with grief over the last days of 'Little Nell'..."

I don't think that writing talent is some ethereal miracle. I think it's at the service of *imagination*. The writer-as-actor, bringing to life vibrant, unified characters, must possess a high degree of imagination. But imagination in itself isn't so rare a quality. The *will* and *discipline* to prod the imagination into searching for the telling details when easier stereotypes beckon—that's the rarity. The difference is always in the willingness to impose upon one's self the discipline. Many people who dismiss themselves as lacking craft or imagination are merely lazy.

A. B. Guthrie had this laziness in mind when he said that "characterizations fall because they ignore, or simplify, the complexity of the human spirit." Guthrie makes these excellent points on character development:

"I think you learn by self-examination. Within you are the seeds, the possibilities, of all the people on the whole face of the earth.... In you are cruelty, rascality, perversion, and, I'll add, the opposite sex. And in you are nobility and goodness and regularity and all the virtues. The one difference between your endowment and that of any of your fellows is one of degree. Some of you won't believe this, but I think it's true. The difference is only one of degree. Man and woman are joined in the human spirit, and villain and hero, and the ugly and the beautiful.

"So learning human nature is learning yourself. So the writing of a novel is self-exploration, self-discovery, self-realization....

"I call this understanding of people through self-knowledge the final feat of the imagination in fiction."

Or, in the words of Guy de Maupassant: "Thus it is always ourselves that we disclose in the body of a king or an assassin, a robber or an honest man, a courtesan, a nun, a young girl, or a coarse market-woman; for we are compelled to put the problem in this personal form: 'If *I* were king, a murderer, a prostitute, a nun, or a market-woman, what should *I* do, what should *I* think, how should *I* act?' We can only vary our characters by altering the age, the sex, the social position, and all the circumstances of life, of that *ego* which nature has in fact enclosed in an insurmountable barrier of organs of sense. Skill consists in not betraying this *ego* to the reader, under the various masks which we employ to cover it."

When a character comes alive as another facet of the author himself, the writer is *compelled* to feel compassion for him or her. Perhaps he's a mass murderer, but he is also the writer, who, unless he's truly insane, will find his motives reasonable and justifiable within the framework of his character's makeup. Perhaps, to use a now trite Freudian approach, every woman he kills is symbolic of his hated mother. Perhaps every man he shoots is the father he hates, but who is still too godlike in his eyes to be attacked directly. The point is that, when the character the writer creates is substantially himself, he can't help but portray him with understanding and empathy, and perhaps love. Although the character may be the villain, he still deserves his day in court—and will get it from a writer who is himself the villian.

Shakespeare understood that. It was his genius. When Shylock, a petty usurer who, because of the insults and humilities directed against him, demands what he believes to be legally his—the right to execute the young man who is his greatest tormentor— Shakespeare allows him this passionate defense of his position:

"He hath disgraced me and hindered me half a million; laughed at my losses, mocked my gains, scorned my nation, thwarted my bargains, cooled my friends, heated my enemies! and what's his reason? I am a Jew! Hath not a Jew eyes! Hath not a Jew ears, hands, organs, dimensions, senses, affections, passions? Fed with the same food, hurt with the same weapons, subject to the same diseases, healed by the same means, warmed and cooled by the same winter and summer as a Christian is? If you prick us do we not bleed? If you tickle us do we not laugh? If you poison us do we not die? *And if you wrong us shall we not seek revenge?...* The villainy you teach me I will execute; and it will go hard but I will better the instruction." (*Merchant of Venice.* III.I.)

The writer-as-actor knows that his characters have strengths and weaknesses, just as he does, and if he—and his characters—think otherwise, he and they suffer self-deception. In every rebirth of ourselves as characters we find complexities and contradictions. The writer tries to be aware of them, because they help to provide the texture and layering of his work. Yet, he will not give all characters *full* development because they're not all central to the story. Secondary characters do not deserve equal space, but they *do* deserve equal *honesty*. Although they don't stay long upon the stage, when they appear, they must not be stereotypes or stick figures. Hints of their individuality always surround them, even if they aren't developed.

In fact, the more memorable characters always have more to them than the writer describes. E. M. Forster said of Jane Austen's characters, they "are ready for an extended life, for a life which the scheme of her books seldom requires them to lead, and that is why they lead their actual lives so satisfactorily." He added, "The test of a round character is whether it is capable of surprising in a convincing way. If it never surprises, it is flat."

Another paradox: Fully developed characters aren't snapshots of real people. In the real world, each single human personality is a universe of unacknowledged contradictions. The skilled writer reduces human nature to consistent and digestible form. By consistent I don't mean that there will be no paradoxes or contradictions, but that the driving passions are reduced to two or three, which may be in conflict. The writer, like the actor, takes on the complex nature of real people, but reveals only that which is essential to literary reality and creative intent.

This *appearance* of reality is of particular importance in dialogue. R. V. Cassill, the gifted author and teacher, suggests that the writer-as-actor should be able to record an approximation of a character's natural speech spontaneously. After he has that down on paper, "Then you can tinker with the approximation like a piano tuner among the strings until you've given the speech its exact and proper note."

But it's a mistake to assume that dialogue on the page should be a faithful rendition of real-life talk. Here's what happens in real conversation:

—We talk and talk, using mountains of unnecessary words.

—Often we don't make our point at all, and when we do, it isn't clear.

—We use incomplete sentences, and such poor construction and grammar that reading what we speak would embarrass most of us.

One reviewer of my McPherson biography, *Least of All Saints*, pointed out that the dialogue of Minnie Kennedy, mother of Aimee Semple McPherson, was unrealistically overburdened with clichés. In fact, several people who had known Minnie personally insisted that she liberally seasoned every conversation with Bible verses and trite expressions. I'd been faithful to reality. But literature conveys the *perception* of reality—something reality itself rarely does because of the complexity. In dialogue a little goes a long way. A few clichés from Minnie when they were truly inappropriate would have done the job, while all of the genuine blabbering appeared to the reader fictional.

I'm not saying that a book can't succeed in spite of unconvincing dialogue. In fact, Robert James Waller's *The Bridges of Madison County* has proven a remarkable success. Yet, Robert Kincaid talks *at* Francesca for page after uninterrupted page as a means of conveying information to the reader, and, later in the book, Francesca does the same. What's more, the style of the dialogue is often interchangeable—only the material of the conversation distinguishes the two characters.

The point: Flaws can be found in virtually every book ever written. If the strengths are great enough, the work can override those faults. But the serious writer must aim for perfection if he is to avoid the mediocre, and ineffective. Unconvincing dialogue can be a glaring and insurmountable imperfection.

Robie Macauley says in his book *Techniques in Fiction* that dialogue should:

Be brief.

Add to the reader's knowledge.

Eliminate the routine exchanges of ordinary conversations, those that go nowhere and mean nothing.

Appear spontaneous.

Contribute to the story's progress.

It should also reveal character and show relationships among people. If it doesn't achieve those ends, no matter how true it rings, or how multi-faceted a diamond it appears to the writer to be, it has no place in the work.

Acting takes courage, whether on stage or on paper, the courage to risk failure and embarrassment, the courage to get out of the safety of the you with whom you're comfortable into a new, perhaps bolder, possibly outlandish self. But, unless you plan to build a career writing reference manuals or telephone directories, you'll have to learn to perform in the theater of the imagination.

And here, I predict, is what you'll discover: Acting is one aspect of writing that never grows tiresome. It's the only way I know to awaken each morning with a fresh perspective, with new challenges, friends and passions. Acting on paper will improve your writing and make it easier. It'll also make life a bit more pleasant. The world of self-exploration always does—even for adults.

CHAPTER VI
The Director's Art

The dramatist, stage manager, set designer, actors—all contribute unique skills without which the production would fail. But none of them, not even the dramatist, carries responsibility for the entire production on his shoulders. The director alone does that. Everyone else works in the heat of his respective passions. The director steps back to view the whole. He *manipulates* passion to achieve his end, but he does so from a cool, detached, objective stance.

In writing, the director is that aspect of the writer's craft which represents discipline. In the beginning, when the first draft is written, the director takes a vacation. His other selves enjoy the freedom of uninhibited creativity. But when the director assumes his position of leadership, he's heartless in his demands. He may remove the others' best-loved passages, declaring that they contribute nothing to the creative intent. The director makes enemies of his other selves, dispassionately shaping the finished work to his highest standards, sacrificing everything to bring it as close as he can to perfection. He pays particular attention to *pacing, freshness, balance,* and *unity.*

Pacing

Every literary effort obviously takes place in an artificial time frame. I spoke earlier of an article I wrote about bicycle racing in America; I used the framework of an actual race at the Trexlertown, Pennsylvania, Velodrome. The article began when the race began and ended when the race ended. Yet, it took a typical reader 20 minutes to complete the article, although the race was over in under five minutes.

The time frame of the article was not true to life. That's obvious when the writer uses subheads like, *Ten years later*. The reader covers those words in a fraction of a second. In real life it takes ten years for ten years to pass. Yet, the writer-as-director makes sure that the artificial time of the story unfolds consistently and believably. That's pacing. Even among the best writers, pacing can be a problem. Henry James, usually a master of pacing, took himself to task concerning his novel *Roderick Hudson*: "Everything occurs none the less too punctually and moves too fast: Roderick's disintegration, a gradual process, and of which the exhibitional interest is exactly that it *is* gradual and occasional, and thereby traceable and watchable, swallows two years in a mouthful, proceeds quite *not* by years, but by weeks and months, and thus renders the whole view the disservice of appearing to present him as a morbidly special case."

Upon first reading of Hemingway's *Old Man and the Sea*, as a high school student, I thought it a crushing, senseless bore. About two-thirds through, I wrote in the margin of my notebook, "So cut the line already and go home!" In fact, the books is a *tour de force* of pacing. In only 130 pages, Hemingway manages to paralyze us with the tedium of the colorless, purposeless, stubborn struggle between a man and an obstacle to his will. It's a far greater achievement than is generally recognized—we're as numb as the old man when the book ends, because we feel that we have spent as much time with that cursed fish as he did.

Henry James felt that the "eternal time-question is accordingly, for the novelist, always there, and always formidable; always insisting upon the *effect* of the great lapse in passage of time." Compressing time, he recognized, although clearly fictitious, is essential to art.

Proper pacing is the illusion that time is moving consistently throughout the work. Usually, the passage of time is relative to space—the number of pages devoted to description. The greater the number of pages, the slower time seems to pass. An author might deliberately devote several pages to description in order to slow the passage of time. Another way to do that is through substories that interrupt the progress of the primary story. Still another approach practiced by writers from Trollope to Maugham: The narrator simply talks to the reader.

Yet, the clever writer can get away with saying, "time passed," by preceding those words with a dramatic episode. For example, Nathanial Hawthorne, in his short story *The Great Stone Face*, announces Ernest's passage from childhood to maturity by writing, "The years went on, and Ernest ceased to be a boy. He had grown to be a young man now." That's not much better than, *ten years passed*, except that, just before those words, Ernest has a disappointing experience.

All his life, he's looked forward to meeting the kind, heroic incarnation of the Great Stone Face which nature has carved into a nearby mountain. But when Ernest meets Mr. Gathergold, who throws copper coins to the masses and is hailed as the Stone Face, his expectations are dashed; he turns sadly toward the valley where, through a gathering mist, he sees on the mountain "those glorious features which had impressed themselves into his soul."

After that dramatic experience, "The years went on."

Gathergold quickly fades into oblivion. Soon the populace declares General Blood-and-Thunder to be its hero, and Ernest, who spends hours each day studying the face in the mountain, longs to meet him. Again he's disappointed.

"Fear not, Ernest," said his heart, even as if the Great Face was whispering to him—"Fear not, Ernest. He will come."

Again, following the dramatic scene, Hawthorne, with literary slight-of-hand, tells us, "More years spun swiftly and tranquilly away. Ernest still dwelt in his native valley and was now a man of middle age."

Yet another candidate for Stone Face appears in the person of Old Stony Phiz, and Ernest, in his eagerness to believe, is almost persuaded that Phiz is the one he seeks. But melancholic and almost despondent, he finally admits that the prophecy remains unfulfilled.

We read then, "The years hurried on, treading in their haste upon one another's heels and now they began to bring white hairs and scatter them over the head of Ernest; they made revered wrinkles across his forehead and furrows in his cheeks. He was an aged man."

In the end, people recognize that Ernest himself, whose life comprised all the many qualities of character and compassion that he had observed in the Great Stone Face, is the mountain's mirror image.

Hawthorne's trick was to precede each large passage of time with a dramatic event. In our own experience, as we look back over time, we realize that, at least in memory, our lives unfold from peak to peak, with years of plains and valleys stretching in between. We are willing to accept the same in literature.

When a story suddenly seems to move faster than it should for no purposeful reason, it's usually because the writer has taken the easy way out. He's come to a scene that he doesn't like writing. Perhaps he doesn't have first-hand experience to draw upon and is unsure how to handle it. Perhaps he *does* have the experience and wants to avoid the pain of reliving the scene. Each of us has known moments that we prefer to keep in the closets of our memory—death-bed scenes, failures, separations. But if we're going to write about these realities—and what else have we to write about?—then we have no choice but to render them fully and honestly. That detail will slow the pacing.

On the other hand, the material sometimes unfolds more slowly than it should. Assuming that the writer understands and strives for consistent pacing, he's probably lost sight of his beacon, his creative intent, and has gone off on tangents. One type of tangent is *discourse*: Writers are thinkers, and thinkers have opinions, and when persons with opinions find a platform from which to express themselves, they can go on and on. Or they may fly off into a frenzy of description or

95

create entire scenes simply because they *like* them. They might add entire chapters that not only fail to enhance development but actually detract from it, as discussed in chapter three.

Pacing problems are natural to the evolution of a literary work, and the writer can tie himself up in knots worrying about them prematurely. The writer-as-director has the overview. He's the one who, during the rewriting, sees to the pacing.

Freshness

Some years ago, Snoopy of Peanuts fame sat at his typewriter and wrote, *"War and Peace,"* then *"East of Eden," "Gone With the Wind." "A Tale of Two Cities."* Finally, frustrated, he threw up his paws and exclaimed, "All the great titles have been taken!"

Likewise, it might seem, as I suggested in chapter three, that all the best settings have already been taken, that the best characters have lived in the pages of books published long ago, that the best phrases have already been turned. But the veteran writer knows that it isn't so. And, unless we start cloning people, it can never be so, for each of us, in our genes and experience, is unique. To illustrate: On the corner of my desk is a houseplant. Because I'm particularly sensitive to the way things *feel*, I might describe its leaves as the dark green of velvet against a lighter shade of satin. But if you're visually oriented you might see those same leaves as the color of a forest floor against ranging fields of clover. If food is important to you, spinach and kiwi might be your metaphors.

The director's job includes spotting the lapses in creativity that all writers experience, when they settle for the overused, the colorless and the lifeless. If we truly believe that all the best titles have been taken, we are fools not to resign the hope of quality writing. Without imagination there can be no talent, no art. The director spots what is old and withered and, through his imagination, makes it young and pink with life.

Some instructors in writing try to teach this infusion of imagination by asking their students to make a list of adjectives and another of nouns, and randomly align words of the first list with those of the second. The purpose is to stimulate fresh approaches to description. That does no harm, but I don't think it does much good, either. We learn to write by writing and reading—it doesn't matter which comes first, but both are essential and both must be pursued continually. The writing improves our insight as readers, and the reading makes us more careful, polished writers. Beyond that, the qualities of freshness which make a work take on vitality and uniqueness can't be found externally, in books like this or from teachers or writing. They're the product of experience and imagination, the realization, for example, that pain has a sound— the dull ache of pounding drums, the sharp slash of a woman's scream. The freshness that makes writing come alive is ultimately the result of conceiving the interconnectedness of things—the color of a touch, the smell of a color, the texture of an odor. Certainly, it can be overdone—that's the point when the imagination calls attention to itself, thereby distracting from the creative intent. More often, it's the sterility of imagination that distracts.

Balance

Balance and pacing differ in this respect: Pacing is a function of time. It has to do with the movement through real and literary time of the entire work.

Balance refers to the *weight* given each of the work's many separate parts. For example, dialogue and narration need to be balanced in quality writing, as compared to the popular novel or story, in which dialogue can continue for pages.

The space and time given to specific characters must also be balanced, relative to their importance. The ones to whom more pages are devoted take on an importance greater than the others. The same is true of various settings. Only the important ones deserve extensive space.

In long, complex books, maintaining balance can be an extraordinary challenge. Yet, when realized, it becomes the hallmark of writing excellence, a symphony of developments and subdevelopments, characters, settings and themes, each in harmony with the other.

But balance in writing isn't achieved by formula. It depends on the writer's own sense of value. It is subjective, and that means it varies writer to writer and era to era. Consider, for example, the "weight" given to a story's moral or creative intent in 19th century literature. Kate Chopin was a gifted, liberated realist, but she drives home the message of some stories so elaborately that contemporary readers might find those words lacking in balance. In "Ma'ame Pélagie," for example, she concludes, "Poor Ma'ame Pélagie! How could it be different! While the outward pressure of a young and joyous existence had forced her footsteps into the light, her soul had stayed in the shadow of the ruin." Had the story ended one paragraph sooner, it would have been perfectly balanced for today's readers.

A more recent writer who's been accused of lacking balance is Flannery O'Connor. Her story "The Artificial Nigger" is a good example. An old man, Mr. Head, goes well beyond repenting the stubbornness that causes him and his grandson a day of confusion, discomfort, and emotional pain when we read:

"Mr. Head stood very still and felt the action of mercy touch him again but this time he knew that there were no words in the world that could name it. He understood that it grew out of agony, which is not denied to any man and which is given in strange ways to children. He understood it was all a man could carry into death to give his Maker and he suddenly burned with shame that he had so little of it to take with him. He stood appalled, judging himself with the thoroughness of God, while the action of mercy covered his pride like a flame and consumed it. He had never thought himself a great sinner before but he saw now that his true depravity had been hidden from him lest it cause him despair. He realized that he was forgiven his sins from the beginning of time, when he had conceived in his own heart the sin of Adam, until the present, when he had denied poor Nelson. He saw that no sin was too monstrous for him to claim as his own, and since God loved in proportion as He forgave, he felt ready at that instant to enter Paradise."

O'Connor's genius is such that the story succeeds as religious literature, like Hawthorne's "Young Goodman Brown." But it does so in spite of its imbalance.

Unity

The director is also responsible for focusing all of a work's parts toward the creative intent. About this, Tolstoy, who wrote perhaps the most sweeping, expansive, novel ever, said, "The most important thing in a work of art is that it should have some kind of focus, i.e. there should be someplace where all the rays meet or from which they issue."

The focus—or unity, or singleness—of the work emanates from the creative intent, but it's wrong to think that the intent is separate from the work. In fact, it *permeates* the work, and actually *is* the work. All the parts fit together, clean and complete, to become the unified statement of intent.

That's why writers rarely like the films that are based on their books—unity of theme is often sacrificed to the story line. If parts of the work weren't essential, the skilled writer wouldn't have included them. To eliminate any part of the work is to mar it.

In the theater of the imagination, the writer does his most difficult work in the role of director. He makes his contribution not in the first draft but in the second, third, fourth and so on. He receives an ad-libbed product of passion and talent, and brutally hacks and whittles it into art. His is the task of making major alterations in conception, pacing, balance, freshness, unity. He alone has a sense of the entire work, and decides whether it succeeds or fails, and where and how. Here the writer exercises dispassionate judgment of his work.

The best writer-as-director is stern with himself, but not rigid in his thinking. He's light-footed. He's agile. It's as though, while most brains are suspended in space by sturdy I-beams, his dangles from elastic bands that allow him flexibility, yet keep him secure in his detached perspective. At his best, he can turn a dismal disappointment into a fine production. But there's another perspective from which the writer must judge his material, that of the audience....

CHAPTER VII
An Audience Of One

When the writer-as-director is finished with whatever major reshaping and overhauling the play requires, it's ready for a dress rehearsal before the writer-as-audience, and the rewriting, or "finishing," that will help it achieve its fullest potential. Exposing to others an original gush of spontaneous writing is like rehearsing a play for the first time on opening night. No serious writer would dream of it. In fact, many professional writers don't want *anyone* except a typist to see a first draft. Its hair is rumpled, jowls sagging, eyes weeping, bones aching and breath smelling. It's just gotten out of bed. It needs to be washed and shaved, its skin tightened and color slapped into it. The bones need clothing.

"My first draft usually has only a few elements worth keeping," says Susan Sontag. "I have to find what those are and build from them and throw out what doesn't work, or what simply is not alive."

"I revise the manuscript until I can't read it any longer," explains Robert Graves, "then I get somebody to type it. Then I revise the typing. Then it's retyped again. Then there's a third typing, which is the final one."

Tolstoy said, "The best writers are always strict with themselves." Goldenweizer, his friend and biographer, has written:

> Unless one has seen [Tolstoy's] incredible work, the numerous passages that are rewritten, the additions and alterations, the same incident being sometimes written dozens of times over, one can have not the remotest idea of this labor...
>
> Yesterday [Tolstoy] spoke of this process of creative work:
>
> "I can't understand how anyone can write without rewriting everything over and over again. I scarcely ever re-read my published writings, but if by chance I come across a page, it always strikes me: all this must be re-written, this is how I should have written it...."

Rewriting is tough work. Many people with phenomenal imagination and adequate craft have accomplished nothing because they've lacked commitment to hard work. They settle for the good enough. They want to get on with other things. The serious writer commits himself entirely to perfecting the work he's undertaken. That makes the difference.

A recent Carnegie Mellon University study found that poor writers made 93 percent of their revisions while writing the original drafts of their papers. Those who typed a second draft made few additional improvements then. Good writers made 30 percent of their revisions on the second draft, sometimes including major rethinking and restructuring. That allowed them to put the idea down quickly, and polish the writing later.

Some people are fortunate enough to have friends who have the skill and desire to criticize rough drafts. Decades after he was recognized as one of literature's greatest artists, Thomas Mann asked friends to read his work, and took their comments seriously. When he was 68 and working on *Doctor Faustus*, he read a section to a friend, who "took issue with the end, the last forty lines, in which, after all the darkness a ray of hope, the possibility of grace, appears. Those lines did not then stand as they stand now; they had gone wrong. I had been too optimistic, too kindly, too pat, had kindled too much light, had been too lavish with the consolation. I had to grant that Adorno's criticisms were justified. The first thing next morning I sat down to a thorough overhauling of the one and a half or two pages and gave them the circumspect form they now have."

Some writers have the good fortune to know someone willing to be the audience at a dress rehearsal and, more importantly, capable of giving useful criticism. Usually, unskilled critics of a beginning writer's efforts do little good and potentially inestimable harm because they aren't sensitive to the writer's creative intent. They might criticize what he's done well and praise what fails, and the novice, insecure in the first place, might take this misguided criticism seriously and accept false conclusions. He's better off receiving *no* criticism other than his own as director and audience than suffering the remarks of the untutored. That's one advantage of writing courses and seminars:

The instructors and leaders can establish the ground rules for student interaction and criticism along lines such as these:

1.) What is the writer attempting to do—what's his creative intent?

2.) How successfully has he achieved that intent?

3.) Within the context of his work, how could he have achieved it more effectively?

4.) Was it worth the trouble—do we care?

A sensitive, knowledgeable outside audience can be invaluable, but the writer himself still must always be his first audience. He needs to be objective—neither so positively biased that he's blind to his faults, nor so critical as to make the work stilted or strangled. A major step in every good writer's development is to become an impartial audience for his own work.

One thing that helps is putting the work aside for a few weeks before rewriting. When we go back, we can read what we *wrote*, not what we meant.

Another technique is to read the work aloud. Eudora Welty does that, and says, "I have learned one important thing from reading aloud: It's a marvelous acid test for right or wrong. You hear every flaw come back to you. You learn things about where to cut, where you've said something more than once. Something may not look unnecessary or redundant on paper; but when you speak it, you know."

Here are some of the things the writer-as-audience looks for:

Unnecessary Words

Whether you read silently or aloud, hunt down those unnecessary words and get rid of them. I've suggested to students that they pay me a dollar for every unnecessary word I find in their "finished" manuscripts. Although I've never received any money, most students do suddenly discover scores of unnecessary words on every page.

Usually, verbose writers simply have chosen the wrong stage manager, or narrative voice, one suffering from pretentiousness. They should find another voice, one that knows how to *simply say it—simply*. Every audience will be grateful.

As Strunk and White explain, "Vigorous writing is concise. A sentence should contain no unnecessary words, a paragraph no unnecessary sentences, for the same reason that a drawing should have no unnecessary lines and a machine no unnecessary parts. This requires not that the writer make all his sentences short, or that he avoid all detail and treat all his subjects in outline, but that every word tell."

An audience is quick to recognize plodding, discursive and dull writing. It applauds what satisfies and forgives minor shortcomings. But bore it with wordiness and it will leave the theater—slam the book or magazine closed and look elsewhere for what it wants. The writer has a right to anger his readers, and even to scold them; his first allegiance is to his own creative intent. But he can't be forgiven a boring production, and that's what wordiness can do.

Unnecessary Passages

Sometimes not just words but entire sentences, paragraphs, and even pages need to be thrown out. That's why Robert Louis Stevenson insisted that the writer must "suppress much and omit more."

"He must omit what is tedious or irrelevant, and suppress what is tedious and necessary... Nothing would find room in such a picture that did not serve, at once, to complete the composition, to accentuate the scheme of colour, to distinguish the planes of distance, and to strike the note of the selected sentiment; nothing would be allowed in such a story that did not, at the same time, expedite the progress of the fable, build up the characters, and strike home the moral or the philosophical design....

"[Unfortunately, all too often] our little air is swamped and dwarfed among hardly relevant orchestrations; our little passionate story drowns in a deep sea of descriptive eloquence or slip-shod talk."

Even outstanding writers may have a tendency to wordiness. Although Chekhov was a great admirer of Gorki, he once wrote to the younger writer:

> You are like a spectator in the theater who expresses his rapture so unreservedly that he prevents both himself and others from listening. Particularly is this lack of restriction felt in the descriptions of Nature with which you interrupt your dialogues; when one reads those descriptions one wishes they were more compact, shorter, put, say, into two or three lines. The frequent mention of tenderness, whispering, velvetiness, and so on, gives to these descriptions a certain character of rhetoric and monotony—and they chill the reader, almost tire him. Lack of restraint is felt also in the descriptions of women...and in the love scenes. It is not vigor nor breadth of touch, but plain unreserve.
>
> Colour and expressiveness in description of Nature are attained only by simplicity, by such simple phrases as "the

sun set," "it became dark," "it began to rain," and so on—and that simplicity is inherent in you to a high degree, rare to anyone among the novelists....

Inconsistent Voice

Another distraction that can sneak into a writer's extended work is a subtle change in narrative voice. That's rarely a problem in the short story and feature article, since they're written rather quickly. But writing a book takes months or years, and the writer's relationship to the work can be influenced by his personal life during that time. Some mornings he bounds from bed frisky and witty; on others he feels irritable. He's self-confident one day, insecure the next, has bouts of eloquence and dullness, and these differences in mood can manifest themselves, if only subtly, in the first draft of his work.

Sometimes, for example, he'll write, "I am," and at others, "I'm." Complex and compound sentences will lilt off his tongue in one chapter, and in another everything will come out stilted and stupid. The writer-as-audience looks for these inconsistencies and rewrites them into a single voice.

He will also be looking for words that are out of character for that voice. Flannery O'Connor once advised a colleague, "I think you ought to go through this book sentence by sentence and...take out such words as *chillily, intoxicatedly*." She also discouraged colloquialisms and slang.

Those words weren't excessive—they were wrong, setting what O'Connor calls a low tone. That's a subtle thing—tone—and inconsistencies in it are more difficult to spot than unnecessary words or passages. The trick is to remember that the narrator or stage manager is always a *fiction*. Just as time, characters, and settings are *illusions* of reality, so is the narrator—even in factual literature. He exists both as a voice to convey a work and a device to create an effect. The narrator must maintain his style of speaking—formal, semi-formal, informal—his vocabulary, his position in relation to the reader (does he address the reader directly as "you," or in the third person?), his degree of intimacy—does he refer to himself in first person? The writer-as-audience carefully listens to every word, for the occasional falseness.

Weak Words

As I said in chapter one, words are an intellectual medium. As such they're a barrier to the emotional experience of literary art. But that's not true of all words. Some are symbols of such powerful ideas or objects that, even lacking context, they evoke response through this association. For example: *blood, genitalia, hate, nigger, compassion, death.*

Language is rich in such emotive words, and one measure of the writer's skill is his instinct for them—if not in the first draft then in the rewriting. Compare the following passages, the first by me and the second by Yukio Mishima:

"By the time the lieutenant had at last drawn the sword across his right side, the cut was shallow. He became sick to his stomach and cried out hoarsely. The wound opened. The lieutenant's head drooped, his shoulders heaved, and his eyes opened to narrow slits."

If you think that was hard to take, you may prefer to skip over the passage as it was written by Mishima (italics are mine.):

"By the time the lieutenant had at last drawn the sword across to the right side of his *stomach*, the *blade* was already cutting shallow and had revealed its *naked* tip, slippery with *blood* and *grease*. But, suddenly stricken by a fit of *vomiting*, the lieutenant cried out hoarsely. The *vomiting* made the *fierce pain* fiercer still, and the *stomach* which had thus far remained firm and compact, now abruptly heaved, opening wide its wound, and the *entrails burst* through, as if the wound, too were *vomiting*. Seemingly ignorant of their master's *suffering*, the *entrails* gave an impression of robust health, an almost disagreeable *vitality* as they slipped smoothly out and spilled into the *crotch*. The lieutenant's head drooped, his shoulders heaved, his eyes opened to narrow slits, and a thin trickle of *saliva dripped* from his mouth."

The passage from "Patriotism," which continues through four pages, is terrifying in its vivid, emotive language. (I've selected one of the less distressful paragraphs.) There's no denying that Mishima's prose speaks directly to the emotion because of the words he uses.

Writing for the Audience

The writer can never forget that he's writing for an *audience*. Hemingway said, "When you first start writing you never fail. You think it's wonderful and you have a fine time. You think it's easy to write and you enjoy it very much, but you are thinking of yourself, not the reader, he does not enjoy it very much. Later, when you have learned to write for the reader, it is no longer easy to write." It gets harder because everything now must be examined through the eyes of that specific audience, must be done to please readers.

Certainly a few writers have created for their own pleasure and no one else's, but the overwhelming majority of the art that we enjoy and celebrate has come from those who identified with readers and who judged their own works from that perspective.

Charles Dickens is one of the most clear-cut examples. He insisted that a dramatic work "can never be the circumscribed domain of a limited portion of intellectuals, but it must appeal to anyone, however humble, with a true sense of the beautiful...."

Dickens, according to a biographer, addressed his art to "the great ocean of humanity." His power "lay in the fact that he expressed with an energy and brilliancy quite uncommon, the things close to the common mind," the mind of "the saint and the sinner, the philosopher and the fool, commonness being that universal thing which loves babies, that fears death; that thing which enjoys Dickens."

The writer is not greater than his public, at least not when judging his own work. Then, as an audience of one, he sits elbow to elbow with the masses.

CHAPTER VIII
The Sound and Music

The best literature is musical. Russian writers have called this quality *instrumentovks*, or "orchestration." English-speaking scholars refer to it as euphony. Music creates the tone that permeates the work, the feeling which, for example, Boris Pasternak gave, through words, to *Dr. Zhivago*, and which film makers captured in *Lara's Theme*. The writer has no trumpets or drums, no flutes or fiddles to call upon. But if he's good he does have cadence, or rhythm, assonance and consonance, onomatopoeia—all that his tools, his words, offer beyond their literal meaning.

The professional writer uses these devices subtly and effectively—indeed, he can't help but use them, for they're inherent in his talent for communication. They're common poetic devices, and some theorists condemn them in prose. Rene Wellek and Austin Warren write in *Theory of Literature*, "The artistic value of rhythmical [and by extension euphonic] prose is still debated and debatable. In accordance with the modern preference for purity in the arts and genres most modern readers prefer their poetry poetic and their prose prosaic." Wellek and Warren conclude, however, that "this is probably a critical prejudice of our time. A defense of rhythmical prose would presumably be the same as a defense of verse. Used well it forces us into a fuller awareness of the text; it underscores; it ties together; it builds gradations; suggests parallelisms; it organizes speech; and organization is art."

Those purists who object to poetic devices in prose have a mistaken understanding of what literature is all about, which is communication—directly, intimately, emphatically, and through *every means available.* One might as well tell a conductor to present the *1812 Overture* without percussion and strings as insist that a serious writer abandon the literary devices—the music—we usually associate with poetry.

In fact, the distinction between the best prose and poetry may actually be synthetic. Goldenweizer tells of playing a Chopin prelude one evening for Tolstoy. When he finished, the great writer exclaimed, "Those are the kinds of short stories one ought to write!"

Read this:

Each of us is all the sums he has not counted:
Subtract us into nakedness and night again,
And you shall see begin in Crete four thousand years ago
The love that ended yesterday in Texas.
The seed of our destruction will blossom in the desert,
The alexin of our cure grows by a mountain rock.
And our lives are haunted by a Georgia slattern,
Because a London cutpurse went unhung.
Each moment is the fruit of forty thousand years.
The minute-winning days like flies buzz home to death,
And every moment is a window on all time.

That's from Wolfe's *Look Homeward Angel,* set as blank verse. Is it now poetry? Is Whitman's "Leaves of Grass" a prose poem or poetic prose? These questions need to be answered by those who catalog such works, but certainly not by the writer, who's free to splash his work with vibrant colors and make of it a painting; or carve and smooth it like the marble of a sculpture. Literature is a *comprising* art, and certainly it embraces the devices of poetry.

The fact is that nearly all writers use the music of their languages, whether consciously or not. And their success or failure to a large degree depends upon whether the music enhances or distracts. Hemingway had so little that the starkness of his style tends to draw attention to itself. In the other extreme, Jack Kerouac sometimes becomes so entranced with the music of his words that their meaning suffers. Euphonic devices should reflect the sense of the material without distracting from it.

Rhythm

We're more aware of rhythm, or meter, in poetry than in prose, which is as it should be. But listen to the passage from James Agee's factual account, *Let Us Now Praise Famous Men:*

"All over Alabama the lamps are out. Every leaf drenches the touch; the spider's net is heavy. The roads lie there, with nothing to use them. The fields lie there, with nothing at work in them, neither man nor beast. The plow handles are wet, and the rails and the frog-plates and the weeds between the ties: and not even the hurryings and hoarse sorrows of a distant train, on other roads, is heard."

First there's the *monotony* of the scene, the still-ness, the dullness. It's reflected in the monotony of Agee's parallel structure: "The roads lie there, with nothing to use them. The fields lie there, with nothing to work in them..."

And there's the hushing of the dew made palpable by the repetitive H sounds; "the spider's net is heavy.... The plow handles are wet.... and not even the hurry-ings and hoarse sorrows of a distant train, or other roads, is heard."

But it's the cadence that I want to stress: "The *plow* handles are *wet/* and the *rails* and the *frog*-plates/and the *weeds* between the *ties/*..." Without effort, anyone reading that passage aloud will natural-ly fall into a cadence that reflects the mood of Agee's words.

The rhythmic, musical quality is what Hawthorne's *Scarlet Letter*, for all its wonder, lacks, and it's why Melville's *Moby Dick* soars. Hawthorne could not have written *Moby Dick*, nor could Hemingway, for neither mastered a cadence equal to the theme of Melville's book, a rhythm that rises and tumbles across great oceans and great themes. For this cadence Melville makes sacrifices. His word choice, diction, and gram-mar all suffer. But Melville understood that words speak merely to the intellect; cadence, like the pipe organs in those early movie houses—and churches even now—tells the audience how to *feel*:

"The warmly cool, clear, ringing, perfumed, over-flowing, redundant days, were as crystal goblets of Persian sherbet, heaped up—flaked up, with rose-water snow. The starred and stately nights seemed haughty dames in jewelled velvets nursing at home in lonely pride, the memory of their absent conquering Earls, the golden helmeted suns! For sleeping man, 'twas hard to choose between such winsome days and such seducing nights. But all the witcheries of that unwaning weather did not merely lend new spells and potencies to the outward world. Inward they turned upon the soul, especially when the still mild hours of eve came on; then, memory shot her crystals as the clear ice most forms on noiseless twilights. And all these subtle agencies, more and more they wrought on Ahab's texture."

And later:

"The whale, the whale! Up helm, up helm! Oh, all ye sweet powers of air, now hug me close! Let not Starbuck die, if die he must, in a woman's fainting fit. Up helm, I say—ye fools, the jaw! The jaw! Is this the end of all my bursting prayers? All my life-long fidelities? Oh, Ahab, Ahab, lo thy work. Steady! Helmsmen, steady. Nay, nay! Up helm again! He turns to meet us! Oh, his unappeasable brow drives on toward one, whose duty tells him he cannot depart. My God, stand by me now!"

Melville's cadence in *Moby Dick* reflects the book's subject as well as any writer has ever managed. You can *feel* the ship slap into ripping waves in the earlier exerpt—and crash through great ones later.

Now, compare that with these passages from Fitzgerald:

"They [two young women] were both in white, and their dresses were rippling and fluttering as if they had just been blown back in after a short flight around the house. I must have stood for a few moments listening to the whip and snap of the curtains and the groan of the picture on the wall. Then there was a boom as Bucannan shut the rear windows and the caught wind died out about the room, and the curtains and rugs and the two young women ballooned slowly to the floor."

And elsewhere in the great Gatsby:

"Her face was sad and lovely with bright things, bright eyes, and a bright passionate mouth, but there was an excitement in her voice that men who cared for her found difficult to forget: a singing compulsion, a whispered 'Listen,' a promise that she had done gay exciting things just a while since and that there were gay exciting things hovering in the next hour."

Here's cadence mirroring the words that produce it: breezy, rippling, bright, and, unlike Melville's cadence, unpredictable.

In his classic biography *Napoleon*, Emil Ludwig frequently uses the staccato, militant cadence of war:

Now, over night, his unbridled imagination wanders across Asiatic deserts, where a stone-heap successfully resisted him; dwells on that old frustrated plan; while his errant thoughts follow the wraith of the Macedonian to the Ganges.

Day dawns. A year ago, on the altar steps in Notre Dame, he had crowned himself with a circlet of gold and laurels. In a fervent proclamation he reminds his soldiers of that day, and concludes with the promise that for this once he will keep out of the firing line.

Never before has history recorded such words uttered by a combat commander. They have always been eager to declare their determination to defy death in the forefront of the battle. Napoleon, whose grenadiers have seen him in twenty fights and regarded him as a heaven-born leader, can venture to tell his men that he will reward their valor by being careful of his own safety.

Although adapting cadence to the mood of a work might seem *in theory* to disrupt the reader, writers—unlike critics—shouldn't waste time pondering theories when obviously any technique is good when it works and bad when it doesn't. Let's suppose, for example, that the year is 1776 and I'm a young colonist who hates British tyranny. I sit down to write a pamphlet urging revolution, and, completely lacking in talent, I begin, "In times such as these the souls of men are burdened, as are those of women and children. Those who are all talk and no action will play the coward, but those who act bravely will be appreciated."

Thomas Paine did it differently. In both word choice and cadence, he talked tough: "These are the times that try men's souls: The summer soldier and the sunshine patriot will in this crisis shrink from the service of his country; but he that stands it now, deserves the love and thanks of men and women."

The meter of that first sentence permits no two ways of speaking. The cadence is unavoidably, "*These are the times that try men's souls.*" Here are the explosive words of an orator. Throughout his speech we hear him pounding the lectern while soldiers march.

Yet, listen to how lilting this same writer's cadence becomes when he is reasoning with a learned audience:

"In the following pages I offer nothing more than simple facts, plain arguments, and common sense; and have no other preliminaries to settle with the reader, than that he will divest himself of prejudice and prepossession and suffer his reason and his feelings to determine for themselves; that he will put on, or rather that he will not put off, the true character of a man, and generously enlarge his views beyond the present day."

The adapting of cadence to subject has just one limitation, and I've already mentioned it: It must work without distracting. It's the same limitation that applies to any aspect of writing—when technique distracts from the creative intent it's bad technique. When cadence becomes so flowing or choppy or anything else that readers become conscious of it, the writer has overreached.

Readers, however, are not clones, with a single set of critical standards and insights. Melville has been criticized for the sacrifices he made, and which were necessary, to maintain the dynamic rhythm of *Moby Dick*. The question, "How much is too much?" is the artist's alone to answer. He knows his intent. His first and most worthy audience is always himself. That means that, if he really prefers the cadence of "the muted iridescence of an early morning sky," and realizes its shortcomings next to "the muted glow of morning," he must follow his own light.

Assonance and Consonance

Assonance is the repetition of vowel sounds—hat and can, nation and incarnate, eleven and egg. The repetition of the same consonants is known as consonance.

Not everyone appreciates assonance and consonance as literary devices. Flaubert had a peculiar attitude toward repetition of any kind. He refused to use the same word twice on a page, and this aversion to repetition led him to say, "When I find an assonance or a repetition in one of my phrases I know that I am ensnared in something false."

But here's how James Agee, a master of the musical in literature, uses assonance and consonance to great advantage:

"New Orleans is staring, rattling, and sliding faintly in its fragrance and in the enormous richness of its lust; taxis are still parked along Dauphine Street and the breastlike, floral air is itching with the stilettos and embroiderings above black blood drumthroes of an eloquent cracked indiscoverable cornet, which exists only in the imagination and somewhere in the past, in the broken heart of Louis Armstrong; yet even in that small portion which is the infested genitals of that city, never free of desire nor of waking pain, there are the qualities of the tender desolations of profoundest night. Beneath the gulf lies dreaming, and beneath dreaming, that woman, that id, the lower American continent, lies spread before heaven in her wealth."

The passage is so rich with the interplay of vowel and consonant sounds that it seems to be more than the unconscious product of genius. Even apart from the meaning of words, feel the *action* in "floral air is itching with the stilettos of black blood drumthroes of an eloquent cracked indiscoverable cornet..." Feel the role of assonance in "waking pain" and "dreaming, and beneath, dreaming."

Thomas Wolfe is among the most lyrical prose writers in the English language. Notice how, in these opening paragraphs of *Look Homeward, Angel*, he uses a ranging cadence that reflects the expansive theme, and consonance to give the writing texture:

"A destiny that leads the English to the Dutch is strange enough; but one that leads from Epsom into Pennsylvania, and thence into the hills that shut in

Altamont over the proud *coral cry* of the *cock*, and the *soft stone smile* of an angel, is touched by that dark *miracle* of chance which *makes* new *magic* in a dusty world.

"Each of *us* is *all* the *sums* he has not counted: subtract us into *nakedness* and *night* again, and you shall *see begin* in *Crete* four thousand years ago the love that *ended yesterday* in *Texas*."

Onomatopoeia

Some *sounds* have become *words* because the sound reflects their meanings. Bells clang or tinkle. Birds chirp and peep. Wolves howl. Winds whistle.

William Styron is particularly adept in the use of onomatopoeia. Here are a few examples from his novel *The Long March*:

—murmurous noise of bees

—sour gloom

—breeziest good will

—thunderheads bloomed.

When Katherine Mansfield tells us in "At the Bay," "Ah-aah! sounded the sleepy sea," we hear the waves through the mist, swelling gently over the sand. "Aah" is what they sound like.

There are limits, of course, to the poetics of prose. For example, I haven't discussed alliteration. Prose readers just won't accept, "Alice always ambles along Albright Avenue." But the objection here isn't so much to the poetic device—no *poet* would write that line, either—but to just plain bad writing.

It's true: Some people are "tone deaf." They have no sense of the music of language. But most of those drawn to writing and literature appreciate the beauty of language, and much of that is in its music. It's an aspect of writing that most professionals take very seriously.

CHAPTER IX
What No One Else Can Do

In the United States alone, at least 50,000 new books are published every year. This year, *Books in Print* will list more than 800,000 titles. Add to that the hundreds of thousands of books published elsewhere, those copied and printed since the dawn of written communication, the millions of manuscripts never published, and then consider this: There are still unique works to be written, but they will never exist unless *you* write them. These are the books—and articles and short stories and essays—that no one else but you can write.

I recognized that fact as a youth of sixteen, when Grandma Bahr told me of an extrasensory experience she claimed to have had during the First World War. I wrote a brief account of her story and sold it immediately to *Fate*. (I'm still not sure whether that first sale was fact or fiction.) I typed it up and sent it because I knew it was what subscribers to *Fate* wanted to read about, and no other writer in the world had access to Grandma's experience.

A few years later, I learned of a thirteen-year-old girl named Ginny Luck. She was the youngest pilot in the United States at the time. I wrote of her experience for *Teen Power*, and it became a cover story. I knew that *Teen Power* readers would like knowing about Ginny, and no one else was likely to write about her.

Those two stories taught me that each of us knows or has experienced things that are virtually unique to us and of interest to others. That in itself can be the basis of a writing career. But it was not until I was 25 years old, having sold a biography, half a dozen short stories, and scores of articles, that I made a second critical discovery. I realized that I didn't have to keep uncovering *new* ideas in order to sell articles, or develop dramatic new plot lines to sell fiction. I found that what is new and interesting to readers need be no more than the perspective which I, personally and uniquely, can bring to it.

The same is true of you. No one in the world is quite like you, speaks with your voice, knows the world through your experience. Here's the dynamic tension of interpersonal relationships: On one level we're all the same; on another we're all different. We hunger for power, we fear extinction, we admire beauty and reason, we are puppets of passion. We are each of us at once insightful and blind, considerate and selfish, heroic and cowardly, tolerant and judgmental, an incalculable sum of positive and negative qualities and characteristics.

Therefore, when we write the truth about ourselves we write about all humankind. What varies is the degree, the measure of each quality and characteristic. The balance is original.

That originality is essential to writing literature. Guy de Maupassant quotes Flaubert as advising him, "If you have any originality, you must bring it out. If you haven't any, then you must acquire some."

Originality, if it's to have the stamina of quality writing, can't be faked. It's not a Madison Avenue gimmick, an Abbie Hoffman *Steal This Book*, or Andy Warhol *a*. It's not external but internal, and comes from what's real and true within the self. To find it means cultivating *honesty, humility, focus, confidence*, and *courage*.

Honesty

Few of us know very much about ourselves. And that's just the way we want it, because the truth can play havoc with the stability of our lives. To illustrate: Some years ago, I had this conversation with a friend and colleague:

Me: Do you believe in God?

John: Yeah, my wife and kids and I go to church every Sunday.

Me: Do you believe in God?

John: (Chuckling) I teach a Sunday school class!

Me: But, do you believe in God?

John: Of *course*... Well, I never thought about it.

Most people use good common sense when it comes to truth, albeit unconsciously: If the truth helps, they go with it; if it hinders, they ignore or deny it. If that sounds skeptical, perhaps it is. At any rate, it's a comfort that the serious writer cannot afford. Originality requires honesty, and honesty requires the ability to think for one's self.

Most people don't do that. The majority accept uncritically the opinion of the subculture to which they belong, perhaps because they *have* no independent opinion, perhaps to avoid conflict with the majority view.

Beyond the peer group outlook, there's the consciousness of the times, and, for serious writers, a *literary* consciousness of the times. When a group of writers shares a perspective or style or both, that widespread consciousness becomes a movement. Many writers are tempted to conform to the movement, sometimes at the cost of personal honesty. On the positive side, conformity enhances the likelihood of being published, since editors and publishers often reject either radically original or "old fashioned" creative intents and styles because, rightly or not, they assume readers will shun them.

On the other hand, the talented writer often unconsciously conveys even his most subtle feelings to his readers, which is why critics may legitimately question the writer's own explanation of what his work is about. Conformity, when it's dishonest, may permeate the work with a feeling of falseness.

Conforming to a contemporary literary consciousness also stagnates the evolution of art. Just as people like Defoe and Fielding, Kate Chopin, Crane and Joyce moved fiction into new, fruitful directions, so today's writers of literature should be expected to do the same. They can do so only by being honest—not to the voice of a subculture or a mass consciousness or even a literary consciousness, but to themselves.

Humility

Honesty begins with humility. Every artist, particularly if he feels his calling early in life, has a sense of destiny or anointing to a literary priesthood. That's narcissism. It declares, "I have the *right* to command the attention of hundreds of thousands, even millions of readers," and it's a blessing because it can prove self-fulfilling: If one is born to write, one had better just get down to business.

But it can also be a curse if not reined in. The *calling* is sacred, not the called. The dedicated writer ought to realize that he's no more special than a talented carpenter. It's not to his credit that he's commissioned to build a cathedral rather than a hut. In the end, his cathedral is no more important than that lowly hut, for if the body isn't sheltered, the cathedral will be empty.

Only insofar as the writer has the humility to objectively recognize his failures can he improve. In fact, most great writers are particularly critical of their own work. Dickens, for example, even heeded the advice of friends and anonymous readers in formulating his plots.

Other writers have destroyed great quantities of work which they considered inferior rather than to sell it for profit. Katherine Anne Porter asked, "Why should I print my studio litter? I haven't published a fraction of what I've written. I have four bushels of manuscripts I've never tried to publish—forty short stories, and five novels I started when I was young and didn't know I was a short story writer."

Novice writers never throw anything away. Every word is a gem, every work an immortal masterpiece. They've not yet honed their critical faculties in order to distinguish between what they *say* and what they *mean*, what those naked words on the page actually communicate. That's certainly understandable in the novice, but its the by-product of pride and blinds the writer to objective evaluation of his work and eventual improvement. At its worst it leads to pretentiousness and literary exhibitionism.

I'm not permitted to print here my favorite example of literary pride, a prose poem called "The Harvest," which was published in a small weekly tabloid distributed in the Pocono Mountains of Pennsylvania; it was accompanied by the warning "Poems and stories are the sole property of the writer and may not be reprinted in any form without permission of the writer." So I won't reprint it, but I will say that its author manages to compare an airliner to a whale, an olive beast, a serpent, a demon, a Trojan horse, a giant, and again a horse.

Actually, the concept of the piece is good. The plane drops off young soldiers in a fertile field of battle as a farmer might plant seeds, and, after a time, comes back to reap the harvest of the dead. But the clutter of exhibitionism, the artifice, the dishonesty of words selected for display—not communication—makes the work unintelligible.

That's a common problem among beginning writers—purple prose or fine writing. It bothered even William Wordsworth, particularly when he found it in poetry. He insisted, "...there neither is nor can be, any *essential* difference between the language of prose and metrical composition [poetry].... They both speak by and to the same organs; the bodies in which both of them are clothed may be said to be of the same substance, their affections are kindred, and almost identical, not necessarily differing even in degree; poetry sheds not tears 'such as angels weep' but natural and human tears; she can boast of no celestial ichor that distinguishes her vital juices from those of prose; the same human blood circulates through the veins of them both."

A more sophisticated version of affectation has to do with symbols. Regardless of the frequent claims of widely recognized writers that they don't consciously seek out symbols, teachers of literature emphasize them so much that beginning writers force synthetic, intellectually contrived symbols into their work. They become another form of dishonesty.

When Ernest Hemingway was asked whether he would admit to using symbolism in his novels, he answered, "I suppose there are symbols since critics keep finding them. If you do not mind, I dislike talking about them and being questioned about them. It is hard enough to write books and stories without being asked to explain them as well. Also, it deprives the explainers of work. If five or six or more good explainers can keep going why should I interfere with them? Read anything I write for the pleasure of reading it. Whatever else you find will be the measure of what *you* brought to the reading."

Hemingway has also said, "I know what I am writing about but I never throw in symbols consciously. Sometimes I find out what I'm supposed to mean when I read the books on my work. I guess somewhere some of the same ideas must be in me. I certainly do have crazy ideas."

Katherine Ann Porter insisted, "Symbolism happens of its own self and it comes out of something so deep in your own consciousness and your own experience that I don't think most writers are at all conscious of their use of symbols. I never am until I see them."

"I really didn't know what a symbol was until I started reading about them," says Flannery O'Connor. "It seemed I was going to have to know about them if I was going to be a respectable literary person."

The writer who consciously invents symbols risks creating parables and allegories rather than quality short stories and novels. The better course is simply to do the writing, steadfastly avoiding symbols. That can lead to at least three potentially positive results:

—He may write fine works in which no one finds symbols.

—He may write fine works in which he has included no symbols; yet, teachers and critics find them anyway.

—He may write fine works in which he has unintentionally infused symbols which he can carefully develop in the rewriting.

Focus

Just as the writer must be honest if he's to be original, he must be focused. The writer at work exists in a world other than the one in which his body dwells. Whether the project is fact or fiction, for the duration of the undertaking the writer is literally "not all there." Nonwriters may not understand such an experience, but an imagined environment can be more real than a literal one. Created characters (or *re*created, in nonfiction), can become so vivid that the events of those lives fill the writer with joy or heartbreak. Focus makes each character *real*. The focused writer looks past the stereotypical qualities to the underlying motives, genetic predispositions and anatomical characteristics which together make each character unique.

The writer also focuses on his own senses. The way they present reality is unique to him—it's what makes his writing original. Willa Cather used the analogy of painters: "What could be more different than Leonardo's treatment of daylight, and Valesquez'? Light is pretty much the same in Italy and Spain—

southern light. Each man painted what he got out of light—what it did to him."

Only you can see things—or hear them, taste, smell, feel them—as you do. That's one of the great pleasures of reading literature: the opportunity to experience things in new ways, as the anointed—as the writer—does. The artist who is focused on the senses might find, for example, a relationship between a pock-marked face, the skin of an orange, and the moon's surface. He might recognize the quality shared by velvet, moss, and peaches. Rotting leaves might smell to him like mushrooms taste, and stars at midnight might look the way ice cubes should when stirred in a crystal goblet.

Confidence

Earlier, I referred to the paradox of the serious writer's personality—he must have humility if he's to grow as an artist, but he also needs a great deal of self-confidence, for, if he's good, he dares to stand emotionally naked before his readers. The painter puts on canvas his interpretation of what he *sees*. The composer records the music he *hears*. But the writer, like the actor, portrays what he *is*. He steps before an audience and strips his emotions bare, for, whatever the names he gives to his characters, whatever person he takes on as narrator, what's displayed is always his own evil, perversion, ugliness, and bleakness as well as his goodness, heroism, and joy.

"No artist can be reproached for shrinking from a risk which only fools run to meet and only genius dares confront with impunity," says Joseph Conrad. He describes writing as "a task which mainly consists in laying one's soul more or less bare to the world...."

For the most part, accomplished writers are friendly, vivacious, entertaining people, but there's no getting around the fact that they have strong egos. They have answers—or think they have—to questions yet unasked, and they don't sit quietly on the sidelines awaiting an opportunity to express them. They generally get along well with those who treat them with deference and are vicious competitors when challenged. They tend not to like other writers because of their competitive natures—consider the unpleasantries that passed between Buckley and Vidal, Capote and Mailer, Defoe and everyone, and the two-faced backbiting gossip among virtually all of the French writers of Flaubert's era. Yet, the sense of self is essential to virtually all artistic achievement, including literary.

Courage

All artists put their talent on the line, to be accepted or rejected by critics and the public. But the writer and the actor do more. They expose the truth not only to their readers, but their deepest selves. Theirs is the courage to be faithful to the truth that's in them. It's a courage that relatively few people have, which is one reason that there are relatively few outstanding writers and actors.

Courage serves the writer in another way: If he's any good, he thinks himself worthy to compete with the greatest of writers. That's what led James Michener to say, "I think about Tolstoy, Flaubert, and Dickens, and I am jealous of what those authors accomplished.... I remain jealous, and this gives me a guide to what I might accomplish. Without that sense of jealousy, of greatness, I doubt that I would have amounted to much."

A couple of decades ago a colleague (who, I tell you gleefully, has amounted to nothing over the years), asked why I was depressed about my career although I was earning royalties from several books and had published in many major American magazines. I told him that my competition was Mark Twain and Herman Melville, that the race had begun and that I was still driving to the track.

"How dare you compare yourself with them?" he demanded. "They're gods!"

"I suppose I believe in myself," I told him.

But that's only half the answer. The writer writes because *he has something to say,* and he is confident in the ultimate fruition of his efforts: The writer needs to believe that his work will be published. In fact, if he's any good, his chances of publishing are probably better than most people think. Every year the large, profit-oriented publishers take on a few new writers; they need to replenish their dying stable of "names." What's more, quality books continue to be published by the many small companies that are providing the only real excitement in the industry today. These entrepreneurs welcome new writers, since most of them pay little or no advance. But they give individual attention to each book, promote it, (which is more than major publishers are likely to do for the works of new writers), and recognize that *their* careers, too, depend upon the success of every work they publish.

The academic presses, too, are dedicated to publishing good books whether or not they're likely to draw a large readership.

Let's assume that a new writer's book eventually appears in print. Now the writer needs still more courage and self-confidence, for he's about to meet the critics. A good critic takes his responsibilities as seriously as a good writer does, but a good critic is every bit as rare as a good writer. For the most part, they are not critics at all but reviewers who would rather be authors if only they had talent. Often they use the forum of the review to display their astounding wit. Since the public applauds insults more readily than compliments, the reviewer who seeks applause above all—including honesty—understandably is disposed to be cleverly destructive.

How else are we to understand this review of Dickens' *Bleakhouse*: "More than any of its predecessors chargeable with not simply faults, but absolute want of construction... meager and melodramatic." (Note the clever alliteration.) Another reviewer wrote, "Last winter I forced myself through this *Tale of Two Cities*. It was a sheer dead pull from start to finish. It all seemed so insincere, such a transparent make-believe, a mere piece of acting." Emily Bronte's *Wuthering Heights* was said to have a thousand times the faults of *Jane Eyre*, "and the only consolation which we have in reflecting upon it is that it will never be generally read."

T. S. Elliot's play *The Cocktail Party* was dismissed as "nothing but a finely acted piece of flapdoodle," and Emerson was called by Carlyle "a hoary-headed and toothless baboon." (For eighty-seven pages of the like, I recommend *Rotten Reviews*, edited by Bill Henderson and published by Penguin Books.)

There are no two ways about it—the serious writer must confront reviews with a closed mind and a sense of humor. Flannery O'Connor once told an interviewer, "Some old lady said that my book left a bad taste in her mouth. I wrote back to her and said, 'You weren't supposed to eat it.'" The same book may be praised by one reviewer and damned by another, and rare is the book that's universally cheered or hissed. Unfortunately, readers believe, often mistakenly, that all reviewers take their responsibilities seriously.

The writer has enough to worry about without letting reviews distract him. Of course, if every reviewer condemns the work for the same reason, that's worth weighing. But in the end, as Tolstoy told his biographer, "I am always saying that a work of art is either so good that there is no standard by which to define its qualities—that is real art—or it is quite bad." He added:

"I think that every great artist necessarily creates his own form also. If the content of works of art can be infinitely varied, so also can their form. Once Turgenev and I came back from the theater in Paris and discussed this. He completely agreed with me. We recalled all that is best in Russian literature and it seemed that in these works the form was perfectly original."

Quality writing is a tough business on every hand. To pay the bills through writing takes not only talent but luck. And why bother? Anyone with the skill, imagination and drive necessary to write professionally can earn six times the money in half the time with one-third the effort in the business world, and have health insurance, paid vacations and a pension plan in the bargain.

But the person born to write won't listen. Perhaps he's already experienced the trance-like hours where he dwells in another existence, hears the people to whom he's given life speak in their own voices, sees them confront and interact with each other. Perhaps he's said to them, "Slow down, I can't write that fast!"

Maybe he already knows the awe and humility of going beyond himself and his abilities, writing things he knows he cannot write, producing depths of feeling and insight that came from who knows where?

If he's felt the joy of conveying what is deepest in him to another human being, then he's lost. One way or another, as a job or a hobby, he will go on because he has had a taste of surpassing his mortality.

CHAPTER X
Opening Night

But there's more to it than that. Irving Wallace asked himself why he continued to write the night before he began *The Prize*:

> Is the challenge undertaken, as so many critics insisted about my previous novel, purely for money? Is it done, as so many professors have said, to find a means of expressing oneself? Is it, as someone has written, an effort to find some degree of immortality? Or is it done, as Dr. Edmund Bergler, the eminent psychoanalyst, stated after he treated thirty-six author-patients, to satisfy a neurotic need for "exhibitionism" "voyeurism" and "masochism?"...

> That same night, late, I also reread sections of a Maugham book, *The Summing Up*: "...He [the writer] does well

only to write to liberate his spirit of a subject that he has so long meditated that it burdens him and if he is wise he will take care to write only for the sake of his own peace.... For the disadvantages and dangers of the author's calling are offset by an advantage so great as to make all its difficulties, disappointments and maybe hardships unimportant."

For the sake of peace, yes. For a purging, for catharsis, yes.

I remembered something I had read in another book, and in the silence of the night in the large house I went to find it. I found it in *Arrow in the Blue* by Arthur Koestler, and now, with the night giving way to the first ray of dawn, I read Koestler:

"I have no idea whether fifty years from now anyone will want to read a book of mine, but I have a fairly precise idea of what makes me, as a writer, tick. It is the wish to trade a hundred contemporary readers against ten readers in ten years' time and one reader in a hundred years' time. This has always seemed to me what a writer's ambition should be."

So: We write to attain immortality. Hemingway said, "From things that have happened and from things as they exist and from all things you know and all those you cannot know, you make something through your invention that is not a representation but a whole new thing truer than anything true and alive, and you make it alive, and if you make it well enough, you give it immortality. That is why you write and for no other reason that you know of."

But we write for other reasons as well. Thomas Mann said that he wrote *The Magic Mountain* as a search for the Holy Grail and "The knowledge and the wisdom, the consecration, the highest reward, for which not only the foolish hero but the book itself is seeking.... It is the idea of the human being, the conception of a future humanity that has passed through and survived the profoundest knowledge of disease and death. The Grail is a mystery, but humanity is a mystery too. For man himself is a mystery, and all humanity rests upon reverence before the mystery that is man."

So: We write to find answers to the great questions, to pay tribute to humankind. But we write for still other reasons. According to Joyce Carol Oates, "...there is no art for art's sake, and never was, but only art as a more conscious, formal expression of a human communal need, in which individuals seem to speak individually but are, in reality, only giving voice and form to the intangible that is in the air around them."

So: We write to give voice to the needs of the masses.

And yet there's more: Fictional author Larry Pressman, in my short story "The Gold Pen," expresses it this way:

"Writing is very hard work, perhaps the hardest in the world. I mean the kind of writing that produces art. The writer as artist is always dissatisfied with his work. Oh, he may sit back and smile and think he's done a pretty good job of it, but tomorrow he'll look at it through the critic's eye and say, 'That word's too warm, the pace is too fast here—too slow there. I should have worked harder!' So, next time the art will be better and

139

the work will always get more difficult. It will get harder and harder, because the artist finds deeper and subtler layers in his art, and each one needs perfecting. At times he feels buried and suffocated under those layers of ideas and words with no sure way out. But he goes back and does it again and again, not because he's a masochist and loves the pain, but because it is as close as mortals get to being God. In fact, the artist is more godly than God, for the life he creates, if he is any good, has meaning."

So: We write for immortality, for understanding of ourselves and others, to glorify and give voice to the masses, to exercise godlike power in bringing order to chaos and meaning to absurdity. But that's too general. It doesn't explain why a serious writer undertakes a *particular* book, story or article. The question isn't, why do people write? The question is, why has that author written *this*? Why was this particular event recounted or story told?

What was the creative intent?

That the answer may not be knowable in some contemporary writing is a telling fact in itself, and helps to explain the void in modern literature. As Anthony Burgess explains:

> The trouble is that novelists nowadays do not care sufficiently or believe enough. Masterpieces spring out of conviction.
>
> Evelyn Waugh's "exuberant men" all had unshakable faith in something—whether in European civilization, Christianity, progress, or even just (as with D. H. Lawrence) the redemptive power of sex. Whether their beliefs can be proved by time to be valid is neither here nor there; it is the conviction that counts, and,

with the conviction the energy that springs from it. Most of the novelists of today do not feel sufficiently *strongly* about anything to be urged into attempting some large-scale work of individual vision which, fusing the comic and tragic in a fresh image of man, shall not merely im-press us, the readers, but radically change our view of life—as *Don Quixote*, and *War and Peace* and *Ulysses* have changed it.

Saul Bellow, in his 1976 Nobel Prize for Literature acceptance speech, said that the basic responsibility of the artist is to provide to "the intelligent public...what it does not hear from theology, philosophy, or social theory, and what it cannot hear from pure science—a broader, more flexible, fuller, more coherent, more comprehensive account of what we human beings are, who we are, and what this life is for."

I believe that the best writers have entered upon a "spiritual" vocation, in the broadest sense, and having nothing necessarily to do with theology. They believe that the reality of life is best interpreted and lived in a particular way, and dramatizing that vision is worth the writer's time and effort. It's what D. H. Lawrence had in mind when he wrote, "...because a novel is a microcosm, and because man, in viewing the universe, must view it in the light of a theory, therefore every novel must have the background or the structural skeleton of some theory of being, some metaphysics. But the metaphysics must always subserve the artistic purpose beyond the artist's conscious aim. Otherwise the novel becomes a treatise."

John Updike puts it this way: "A church is a little like a novel in that both are saying there's something very important about being human.... Writing, after all, is an otherworldly thing to do for rewards that may or may not be material. This, in a way, relates to having faith that things will work out, that there is purpose to your life."

"Religion and art spring from the same root and are close kin," says Willa Cather. Tolstoy believed, "Art is the expression of feeling, and the higher it is the greater the public which it can draw to itself. Therefore the highest art must reflect those states of mind which are religious in the best sense of the word, as they are the most universal and typical of all human beings."

This perspective wasn't controversial among the most frequently read and enduring writers of the past; it's become controversial during the twentieth century in part because many people misunderstand the concept of the religious in art. As I've said, it may have nothing to do with doctrine, theology, or "God." It's the intangible framework that gives the artist's vision its vitality, structure, and meaning. Whether the musician portrays that vision in soaring musical crescendos or the painter does so in interrelated abstracts on canvas, whether he implies it in the despair of the Realists or the optimism of the Romantics, his work, if it is well executed, will stand apart for its reaching beyond the temporal.

The accomplished writer offers his own personal faith to his readers. He may be a prophet of damnation like Sinclair Lewis and Stephen Crane, a zealous evangelical like Plato and Nietzsche, or a gently edifying pastor like Eudora Welty and Katherine Anne Porter.

He offers what he has learned of life because he cares about people. A middle-aged would-be writer once told me, "I love the human race—it's the *people* I can't stand." But the writer and his readers are soul-mates. They may share intimacies that neither may be able to discuss with other human beings. He knows that his readers are comrades, seeking to learn from him.

A common characteristic of young writers (I don't mean inexperienced ones) is an obsession with themselves. That was true in the early works of Capote, Vidal, Wolfe, Kerouac, and many others. Self-absorption is proper in youth. But mature writing means getting beyond the self, recognizing and appreciating what is unique and wonderful in others. This fondness for his readers is often behind the writer's creative intent. He wants to help.

Willa Cather says that, just before beginning *The Professor's House*, she saw an exhibition of old and modern Dutch paintings. Many were of living rooms warmly furnished or kitchens full of food and copper pots. But "in most of the interiors, whether drawing room or kitchen, there was a square window, through which one saw the masts of ships or a stretch of grey sea. The feeling of the sea that one got through those square windows was remarkable, and gave me a sense of the fleets of Dutch ships that ply quietly on all the waters of the globe—to Java, etc."

In the book, she created just such a window in a house otherwise overcrowded and stuffy with new things. "I wanted to open the square window," she says, and "let in the fresh air that blew off Blue Mesa and the fine disregard of trivialities which was in Tom Outland's face and in his behavior."

That's what the writer does—he opens the curtains to show what exists beyond the immediate. But in doing that, he does everything. Chekhov wrote:

"Remember that the writers whom we call eternal or simply good and who intoxicate us have one common and very important characteristic: they get somewhere and they summon you there, and you feel not with your mind, but with your whole being, that they have a certain purpose, and like the ghost of Hamlet's father, do not come and excite the imagination for nothing. Some—it depends upon their calibre—have immediate objects: abolition of serfdom, liberation of the country, politics, beauty or simplicity, vodka, like Denis Davydod; others have remote aims, God, the life beyond, the happiness of mankind, and so on. The best of them are realistic and paint life like it is, but because every line is permeated, as with a juice, by awareness of a purpose, you feel, besides life as it is, also life as it ought to be, and this captivates you."

Chekhov agonized endlessly over his own philosophical sterility and that of his contemporaries: "We paint life as it is, and beyond that...even if you lashed us with whips we could not go. We have neither immediate nor remote aims, and in our soul—a great emptiness. We have no politics, we do not believe in revolution, we have no god, we are not afraid of ghosts, and I personally have no fear even of death and blindness. He who desires nothing, hopes for nothing, and is afraid of nothing, cannot be an artist."

That was Saul Bellow's complaint as well:

"Yes, and we modern writers are not really prepared to deal with these ultimate questions, and this is one reason why literature has been forced back, and has allowed itself to be forced back into trivialities. A great misfortune. For once you have decided to become a writer of fiction, you have assumed responsibility even as a craftsman to determine whether you are really obliged to accept such cruel restrictions of subject, whether you are going to go on picturing reality as your trade has defined it for you. These trade definitions (every writer knows what I mean) make dull reading, I tell you that. I would rather be a computer programmer than operate in this way."

Yes, the writer who has nothing to say is sure to say it. A few examples of the literature of hopelessness will remain with us more or less permanently, both as curiosities and for their historic significance, just as many useless gadgets are on permanent display in the Smithsonian Institution. For some years they'll continue to be taught because they do represent, almost uniquely in literature, a world view void of meaning and human spirit—or, if you prefer, the will to aspire. But not one of these works is likely to be celebrated as great literature a few decades from now, and that's not because they're tragic—Shakespeare writes tragedy—but because their vision of humankind is whimpering and cringing and terrorized.

That's not the vision of lasting prose. The Hemingways celebrated the unreasoning courage of the individual; the Steinbecks have found slim but real hope in mutual compassion. Even the Joyce of "The Dead" discovered something approaching salvation in the ecstasy of shared love. And O'Connor found it in Christ.

Katerine Anne Porter told an interviewer, "But I tell you, nothing is pointless, and nothing is meaningless if the artist will face it. And it's his business to face it. He hasn't got the right to side-step it like that. Human life itself may be almost pure chaos, but the work of the artist—the only thing he's good for—is to take these handfuls of confusion and disparate things, things that seem to be irreconcilable, and put them together in a frame to give them some kind of shape and meaning. Even if it's only his view of a meaning. That's what he's for—to give his view of life.

"The great writer assuages and palliates some unanalyzable wisdom and knowledge. They hearten us and reinforce our belief that life is rich, curious, and inexhaustible."

One evening some years ago, I sat in a leather chair in the book-lined study of my home deep in the woods of Northeastern Pennsylvania. A single lamp illuminated the room. Classical music played softly on the phonograph while, in other parts of the house, my wife and son and daughter slept. I had just finished writing a book earlier in the day, and, as always after the completion of a months-long effort, I felt as though the work had abandoned me, taking with it vital parts of myself. On the verge of depression, I imagined hearing Chekhov say, "Writing gives me nothing but twitches!"

In my fancy, Flaubert choked back a tear—the perfect phrases kept eluding him. Joyce cursed furiously. Whitman only chuckled—it was all the same to him. "I am great," he said, "I contain multitudes."

I closed my eyes and invited into the room the ghosts of all the writers who ever lived, celebrated and unknown, brothers and sisters who had in common all that accompanies the anointing. Why did they endure it?

"Compelled to it."

"Compelled!" But to what?

To perfecting the art. Yes, Tolstoy was right. In the end, what matters is doing it better and better *for ourselves*. We create art that *we* can love and applaud, that says what *we* want said, and it's the *process* of perfecting the work that counts, the growth and the aspiring to greater growth.

In the spring of 1991, a 58-year-old country singer named Dottie West had struggled against illness and despair to re-establish her career. During a television entertainment program one evening, an interviewer asked, "Dottie, what was your best song ever?"

"I haven't sung my best song yet," she said. That was a week before she died.

Bibliography

Chapter I

Amerongen, J. B., *The Actor in Dickens* (New York: Benjamin Blom, 1969), 27.

Cather, Willa, *Willa Cather on Writing* (New York: Knopf, 1949), 103.

Eckstein, Gustav, *The Body Has a Head* (New York: Harper & Row, 1970), 660-661.

Fontaine, Andre and William A. Glavin, Jr., *The Art of Writing Nonfiction* (Syracuse, New York: Syracuse University Press, 1987), 1.

Mann, Thomas, *Stories of Three Decades* (New York: Modern Library, 1936) 30.

Maugham, W. Somerset, *The Art of Fiction* (Garden City, New York: Doubleday, 1948), 83.

Prenshaw, Peggy Whitman, ed., *Conversations with Eudora Welty* (Jackson, Mississippi: University Press of Mississippi, 1984), 169.

Wallace, Irving, *The Writing of One Novel* (New York: Simon & Schuster, 1968) 58-59.

Chapter II

Ardrey, Robert, *The Hunting Hypothesis* (New York: Atheneum, 1976), 1.

Bradbury, Ray, *Dandelion Wine* (New York: Knopf, 1981), 4.

Cowley, Malcolm, "Storytelling's Tarnished Image) *Saturday Review* 54 (25 September 1971), 25.

Elwood, Maren, *Characters Make Your Story* (Boston: *The Writer* 1973), 11.

Evans, I. O., *Jules Verne and His Work* (New York: Twayne, 1966), 128.

Faulkner, William, *Light in August* (New York: Random House, 1959), 1.

Forster, E. M., *Aspects of the Novel* (New York: Harcourt, Brace & World, 1955), 26.

Hayes, John P., "More Michener," *Writer's Digest* (February, 1985), 31.

Isherwood, Christopher, *A Single Man* (New York: Simon & Schuster, 1964), 1.

Mann, Thomas, *The Magic Mountain*, trans. H. T. Lowe Porter (New York: Knopf, 1961), 603.

Millet, Kate, *The Basement* (New York: Simon & Schuster, 1979), 11.

Plimpton, George, "Conversations with Ernest Hemingway," *Paris Review* n.5 (Spring 1958), 115.

Plimpton, George, ed., *Writers at Work: The "Paris Review" Interviews* (London: Secker & Warburg, 1976), 190.

Porter, Katherine Anne, *Katherine Anne Porter: Conversations*, ed. Joan Givner (Jackson, Mississippi: University Press of Mississippi, 1987), 88.

Stevenson, Robert Louis, "A Humble Remonstrance," in *Memories and Portraits* (Boston: Small, Maynard & Co., 1907), 225-255.

Talese, Gay, *The Kingdom and the Power* (New York: World, 1969), 1.

150

Chapter III

Forster, E. M., *Aspects of the Novel* (New York: Harcourt, Brace & World, 1927), 30-31.

Fugate, Francis L., *Viewpoint: Key to Fiction Writing* (Boston: The Writer, Inc., 1968), 53.

Gide, Andre, *The Journals of Andre Gide*, trans. Justin O'Brien, Vol. 3 (New York: Knopf, 1949), 361-362.

Hardy, Florence Emily, *The Early Life of Thomas Hardy 1840-1891* (New York: Macmillan, 1928), 138.

Maddux, Rachel, *A Walk in the Spring Rain* (Garden City, New York: Doubleday, 1966), 30-31.

Mann, Thomas, *The Genesis of a Novel*, trans. Richard and Clara Winston (London: Secker & Warburg, 1961), 28-29; 128.

Maugham, W. Somerset, *The Art of Fiction* (Garden City, New York: Doubleday, 1948), 46-47; 316.

Strunk, William, Jr. and E. B. White, *The Elements of Style*, 2nd ed. (New York: Macmillan, 1979), 69.

Wells, H. G., *The History of Mr. Polly* (New York: Duffield and Co., 1909), 4-5, 11-13.

Williams, Tennessee, ed. J. Gaines, "Talk About Life and Style with Tennessee Williams," *Saturday Review* 55 (29 April 1972), 28.

Chapter IV

Cassill, R. V., *Writing Fiction*, 2nd ed. (Englewood Cliffs, New Jersey: Prentice-Hall, Inc., 1975), 22.

Cather, Willa, *Willa Cather on Writing* (New York: Knopf, 1949), 35-37.

Fitzgerald, F. Scott, *The Great Gatsby* (New York: Charles Scribner's Sons, 1953), 2.

Hardy, Thomas, *The Return of the Native* (New York: New American Library, 1959), 12-13.

Joyce, James, *Letters of James Joyce*, ed. Stuart Gilbert (New York: Viking, 1966), 273.

Mansfield, Katherine, *The Short Stories of Katherine Mansfield* (New York: Ecco Press, 1983), 263-264.

Prenshaw, Peggy Whitman, ed., *Conversations with Eudora Welty* (Jackson, Mississippi: University of Press of Mississippi, 1984), 3; 81-82

Rice, Anne, *Interview with a Vampire* (New York: Knopf, 1976), 73.

Stevenson, Robert Louis, "A Gossip on Romance," in *Memories and Portraits* (Boston: Small, Maynard & Co., 1907), 218-219.

Tchekhov, Anton, "A Letter to his Brother (10 May 1886)," in *The Life and Letters of Anton Tchekhov*, trans. and eds. S. S. Koteliansky and Philip Tomlinson (New York: Benjamin Blom, 1965), 78-79.

White, James P., and Janice L. White, *Clarity: A Text on Writing* (Los Angeles: Paul Hanson, 1981), 88.

Chapter V

Amerongen, J. B., *The Actor in Dickens* (New York: Benjamin Blom, 1969), 41.

Bahr, Robert, "They Won Without Steroids," *Boys' Life* (July 1977), 76.

Bahr, Robert, "From Crud to Chrome," *Popular Mechanics* (July 1977), 76.

Bahr, Robert, *The Blizzard* (Englewood Cliffs, New Jersey: Prentice-Hall, Inc., 1980), 3-4.

Bahr, Robert, "High School Sex," *Valley Monthly* (February 1978), 26, 29.

Cassill, R. V., *Writing Fiction*, 2nd ed. (Englewood Cliffs, New Jersey: Prentice-Hall, Inc., 1975), 31.

"Confessions of George Simenon," *MD* (March 1969), 225.

Eric, Lozen, "Leaving Home: Is It Easier for Birds?" *Mature Health* (October 1989), 65.

de Maupassant, Guy, "Of 'The Novel,'" Prerface to *Pierre & Jean*, trans. Clara Dell (New York: P. F. Collier & Son, 1902), lvi.

Forster, E. M., *Aspects of the Novel* (New York: Harcourt, Brace & World, 1955), 78.

Guthrie, Alfred Bertram, "Characters and Compassion," *Writer* 62, N. 11 (November 1949), 359.

Hesse, Hermann, "Prologue," in *Demian* (New York: Bantam Books, 1968), 3.

James, Henry, *The Art of the Novel* (New York: Charles Scribner's Sons, 1962), 47.

Macauley, Robie, *Technique in Fiction* (New York: Harper & Row, 1964), 56.

Pollack, Jack Harrison, *Dr. Sam an American Tragedy* (Chicago: Henry Regnery Co., 1972), xi.

Rogers, Lynne, *The Loves of Their Lives* (New York: Dell, 1979), 13.

Chapter VI

Chopin, Kate, *The Awakening and Selected Short Stories* (New York: Bantam, 1988), 173.

Goldenweizer, A. B., *Talks with Tolstoy*, trans. S. S. Koteliansky and Virginia Woolf (New York: Horizon Press, 1966), 74.

Hawthorne, Nathaniel, "The Great Stone Face," in *Stories to Remember*, Vol. 1 (New York: Doubleday, 1956), 264.

James, Henry, *The Art of the Novel* (New York: Charles Scribner's Sons, 1962), 12.

O'Connor, Flannery, *A Good Man is Hard to Find and Other Stories* (New York: Harcourt, Brace & World, 1955), 128-129.

Chapter VII

Amerongen, J. B., *The Actor in Dickens* (New York: Benjamin Blom, 1969), 195.

Goldenweizer, A. B., *Talks with Tolstoy*, trans. S. S. Koteliansky and Virginia Woolf (New York: Horizon Press, 1969), 182.

Hotchner, A. E., "This Week," *Herald Tribune* (18 October 1959). 10-11, 24-26.

Mann, Thomas, *The Genesis of a Novel*, trans. Richard and Clara Winston (London: Secker & Warburg, 1961), 176-177.

Mishima, Yukio, (Patriotism," in *Death in Midsummer and Other Stories* (New York: New Directions, 1966), 115.

O'Connor, Flannery, *The Correspondence of Flannery O'Connor and the Brainard Cheneys* (Jackson, Mississippi: University Press of Mississippi, 1986), 148.

Prenshaw, Peggy Whitman, ed., *Conversations with Eudora Welty* (Jackson, Mississippi: University Press of Mississippi, 1984), 269.

"Story Ideas," Carnegie Mellon, Department of Public Relations (April 1987).

Stevenson, Robert Louis, "A Note on Realism," in *Essays and Criticisms* (Boston: Small, Maynard & Co., 1907), 219-220.

Strunk, William, Jr. and E. B. White, *The Elements of Style*, 2nd ed. (New York: Macmillan, 1979), 23.

Tchekhov, Anton, *The Life and Letters of Anton Tchekhov*, trans. and eds. S. S. Kotelliansky and Philip Tomlinson (New York: Benjamin Blom, 1965), 261.

Wordsworth, William, "The Thorn," in *English Romantic Writers*, ed. David Perkins (New York: Harcourt, Brace & World, 1967), 198.

Chapter VIII

Agee, James and Walker Evans, *Let Us Now Praise Famous Men* (Boston: Houghton Mifflin, 1980), 44-45.

Fitzgerald, F. Scott, *The Great Gatsby* (New York: Charles Scribner's Sons, 1953), 8.

Goldenweizer, A. B., *Talks with Tolstoy*, trans. S. S. Koteliansky and Virginia Woolf (New York: Horizon Press, 1969), 161.

Ludwig, Emil, *Napoleon*, trans, Eden and Cedar Paul (New York: Boni & Liveright, 1926), 242-243.

Maugham, W. Somerset, *The Art of Fiction* (Garden City, New York: Doubleday, 1948), 181.

Melville, Herman, *Moby Dick* (W. W. Norton & Co., 1967), 111-112.

Paine, Thomas, "The American Crisis," in *The American Tradition in Literature*, ed. Sculley Bradley et.al., rev.ed., Vol. 1 (W. W. Norton & Co., 1962), 260.

Wellek, Rene, and Austin Warren, *Theory of Literature*, 3rd ed. (New York: Harcourt, Brace & World, 1956), 165; 162-163.

Wolfe, Thomas, *Look Homeward Angel* (New York: Charles Scribner's Sons, 1957), 3.

Chapter IX

Amerongen, J. B., *The Actor in Dickens* (New York: Benjamin Blom, 1969), 9.

Cather, Willa, *Willa Cather on Writing* (New York: Knopf, 1949), 124.

Conrad, Joseph, "Preface," to *A Personal Record* (Garden City, New York: Doubleday, Doran & Co., 1931), xviii.

de Maupassant, Guy, "Of 'the Novel,'" Preface to *Pierre & Jean*, trans. Clara Dell (New York: P. F. Collier & Son, 1902), lx.

Fugin, Katherine, et al., "An Interview with Flannery O'Connor," *Censer* (Fall 1960), 30.

Goldenweizer, A. B., *Talks with Tolstoy*, trans. S. S. Kobeliansky and Virginia Woolf (New York: Horizon Press, 1969), 57.

Hayes, John P., "More Michener," *Writer's Digest* (February 1985), 31.

Plimpton, George, "Conversations with Ernest Hemingway," *Paris Review* n.5 (Spring 1958), 120.

Porter, Katherine Anne, *Katherine Anne Porter: Conversations*, ed. Joan Givner (Jackson, Mississippi: University Press of Mississippi, 1987), 63.

"Ripley: Books are like Products," *Mobile Press Register* (24 September 1991).

Rotten Reviews A Literary Companion, ed. Bill Henderson (New York: Penguin Books, 1987), 32.

Wordsworth, William, "Preface, Second Edition of the Lyrical Ballads," in *English Romantic Writers*, ed. David Perkins (New York: Harcourt, Brace & World, 1967), 324; 322.

"Writers are Really Servants of Reality," *U. S. News & World Report* (20 October 1986), 67.

Chapter X

Burgess, Anthony, *The Novel Now* (New York: W. W. Norton & Co., 1967), 18-19.

"Saul Bellow: Storyteller," *MD* (October 1982), 186.

Cather, Willa, *Willa Cather on Writing* (New York: Knopf, 1949), 27; 31-32.

Goldenweizer, A. B., *Talks with Tolstoy*, trans. S. S. Kobeliansky and Virginia Woolf (New York: Horizon Press, 1969), 41.

Lawrence, D. H., "Study of Thomas Hardy," in *Selected Literary Criticism*, ed. Anthony Beal (London: William Heinemann, 1955), 188.

Mann, Thomas, "Epilogue," in *The Magic Mountain*, trans. H. T. Lowe Porter (New York: Knopf, 1961), 729.

Oates, Joyce Carol, "New Heaven and Earth" *Saturday Review* (4 November 1972), 51.

Porter, Katherine Anne, *Katherine Anne Porter: Conversations*, ed. Joan Givner (Jackson, Mississippi: University Press of Mississippi, 1987), 88.

Simmons, Maggie, "Free to Peel" *Quest* (February/March 1979), 33; 32.

Tchekhov, Anton, *The Life and Letters of Anton Tchekhov*, trans. and eds. S. S. Koteliansky and Phillip Tomlinson (New York: Benjamin Blom, 1965), 83; 211.

Tenant, Stephen, "An Introduction," in *Willa Cather on Writing* by Willa Cather (New York: Knopf, 1949), xvi.

"Writers are Really Servants of Reality," *U. S. News & World Report* (20 October 1986), 67.